OUT OF THE SHADOWS

The inspiring story of a life-long struggle to overcome shocking sexual and physical abuse at an English Catholic Approved School

DAVID ARMSTRONG

With an Introduction by
John Armstrong

www.tagmanpress.com

Out of the Shadows

First published in Great Britain on 5 June 2014 in original trade paperback format by Tagman Press Ltd.

Tagman Press Ltd.
8 Bridge Court Fishergate, Norwich, NR3 1UE
Tel: 0845 644 4186 www.tagmanpress.com
email:info@tagmanpress.com

© Copyright 2014 by David and John Armstrong

The right of David Armstrong to be identified as the author of this work has been asserted by them in accordance with the Copyright, Designs & Patents Act 1988.

All rights reserved. No part of this publication may be reproduced, stored in a retrieval system or transmitted in any form or by any means, electronic, mechanical, recording or otherwise, without the prior written permission of the authors and copyright holders.

ISBN
E-book 978-1-906749-27-9
Trade Paperback 978-1-906749-26-2

A CIP catalogue record for this book is available from the British Library

Edited by: Helen Hart and Anthony Grey
Cover Design: Graham Watering

Printed by The Really Useful Print Company, Unit 15, Bessemer Road, Norwich NR4 6DQ
Tel: 01603 629796

www.tagmanpress.com

Contents

page

Introduction by John Armstrong 5

Author's Preface 9

Illustrations 68-77

Part One - In The Beginning
page 10

Chapter 1	Happy Days on the Farm 13
Chapter 2	Arrested Aged Thirteen, 1960... 17
Chapter 3	St Vincent's... 21
Chapter 4	Christmas at Home 31
Chapter 5	Back to Hell 35
Chapter 6	Abuse without Boundaries.. 41

Part Two - Out of Control
page 44

Chapter 7	Sent to Prison Aged Fourteen 47
Chapter 8	Life in Prison 49
Chapter 9	Crack-Up 61
Chapter 10	Back Home 65
Chapter 11	Back to Prison... 79
Chapter 12	Off to the Cuckoo's Nest 83
Chapter 13	Block Six Dungeons 89

Contents *continued*

Part Three - Dreams Can Come True
page 102

Chapter 14	My Life Gets Better	105
Chapter 15	Self Re-education	107
Chapter 16	A Late Aberration	111
Chapter 17	Reflections in Tranquility	117
Chapter 18	The Truth About the Catholic Church	123

Postscript 131
Acknowledgements 135
Epilogue by Anthony Grey 139
Bibliography 146

INTRODUCTION
by
John Armstrong

On a bright Sunday afternoon in the autumn of 1947 the sun shone through the stained glass windows of St. John's Roman Catholic church on Earlham Road in Norwich, brilliantly illuminating the baptismal font and the gilded crucifixes above the high altar. I watched Father Anthony Roberts cradling a new-born infant in one arm as he gently sprinkled holy water from the font with his other hand onto the sleeping child's forehead.

'I baptise thee David Michael Hammond," he said quietly, "in the name of the Father, the Son and the Holy Ghost."

The Armstrong family, myself then aged fifteen, my older sister Constance, who is David's mother, and his Irish father Sean Hammond, and other uncles and aunts and friends stood reverently in a formal circle, dressed in our Sunday best. The ladies wore flowered hats and cotton dresses, the men and boys were dressed in smart suits and black polished shoes, smiling proudly. At the end of it all, my nephew David had become a true Catholic boy.

After the service we made our way quietly home on a red double-decker bus travelling eastwards along Dereham Road out of the city. Nanny Armstrong had set out a lovely tea on the back of a well-trimmed lawn behind our council house home on the Larkman Lane housing estate at the western edge of Norwich. There were sandwiches of potted meat and Grade A tinned salmon for all, washed down with cups of sweet sugared tea followed by cakes, jelly, blancmange and cream.

It was a day of family reunion, love, warmth and happiness. David, I remember gurgled and smiled contentedly in my sister's arms throughout. I had seen him for the first time a few weeks earlier just minutes after he was born in the same house. His birth had made me an uncle for the first time at the tender age of fifteen, so it was a very special occasion for me too. All round it was a truly happy celebration.

We could never have imagined then in our wildest dreams, what agonies lay not very far ahead for David. Events beginning just thirteen years later would be connected directly to the institution of the Roman Catholic Church into which he had just been so movingly baptised and christened. For years David was to suffer in silence many indignities and deep physical and psychological pain, without revealing much detail to anyone, even those closest to him. These events, when eventually known, would come to sicken and horrify us – but all that has only come to light in full very recently, nearly half a century after it happened.

In fact David 'comes out of the shadows' fully here for the first time, revealing the detailed psychological and physical damage inflicted on him, that was to have enduring lifelong effects. But he does this always with a quiet dignity, without any evident self pity or paranoia, referring modestly to repeated physical and sexual abuse, vilification and sadism carried out by a so-called Christian Brotherhood in a Catholic "approved school" institution in Dartford Kent, over a period of a year.

This first year was followed by some months in Norwich prison, two further years in a Borstal home, and ultimately two more years in Broadmoor, the state-run mental hospital for the criminally insane. In a rational world, thirteen year-old David should never have been sent to the approved school in the first place for a very minor and unknowing infringement of the law. And certainly he should never have then been later sent on to Borstal, let alone be committed finally to the extremes of Broadmoor. In both Borstal and Broadmoor, the effects on him of his first year's expereince at the age of thirteen were greatly exacerbated until a discerning psychiatrist virtually saved his life and sanity by recognising he should never have been there in the first place.

Not the least interesting aspect of his story are his descriptions of his prolonged encounters within Brodmoor's walls and dungeons with Jimmy Savile, the late disc jockey who in the past year or two has become the focus himself of an enormous array of sexual abuse allegations. David began work on this book long before the Jimmy Savile scandal became public knowledge. The enormous media attention given to it and similar accusations against many other radio and television broadcasters have focussed greater attention on this subject in Britian perhaps than ever before. So seemingly by chance, David's story has taken on a new contemporary relevance. But here Jimmy Savile figures more as hero than villain.

To his great credit, David relates all these things dispassionately and leaves no stone in his story unturned. And it is triumphantly in the end a story of courage, fortitude, hope and eventually to David's great credit, forgiveness – and indeed a fine example of the power of the human spirit to overcome adversity and survive.

The reason he has written and revealed his full story at long last is not out of spite, hate, malice or vengeance - and he has certainly not done it for financial gain. His sole purpose, I am sure, is solely to reveal his childhood experience and expose the truth. Because he and thousands of other little mites like him were baptised and educated into the Catholic Church system, and he wants to reveal to the world how power can corrupt, and how the sadistic, psychologically twisted minds of members of certain religious orders and their perverted acts could be covered up for their own gain and power.

For my dear nephew David to put on record for all to see, details of the cruel tortures he suffered takes much courage, and I admire him unreservedly. I am his closest relative – and by the way we feel more like brothers to each other than uncle and nephew – so we have often talked of these things at length. And we decided we wished above all else to help those thousands of children in Catholic-run institutions who have suffered similar experiences. It is our hope that they too will come forward and speak out – and seek help to tell their stories of what terrible power such religious institutions have wielded. We also want to put on record that in no way do we want or intend to belittle or condemn those decent good folk - and there are many - who have a genuine faith and find solace in their own beliefs without harming others. For us to do so unintentionally would defeat our own honourable intentions. We only want to reveal the truth. The Catholic Jesuit priesthood have long famously said worldwide : 'Give me the child, and we will give you the man.'

Well, well, well ... in our family that has certainly not been honourably the case.

AUTHOR'S PREFACE

'If good men stay silent, evil will prevail', is a famous quote by Edmond Burke, which encapsulates the primary reason I am sharing my story publicly for the first time. In these pages I bare my soul; I reveal the atrocities I suffered and felt shamed by, to put them on record for all to see. It is my heartfelt wish that my story will encourage other victims, who suffered abuse as children in Catholic-run institutions, to come forward and speak up. Their truths would not only support others who have done so, but I believe from my own personal experiences that to talk about the trauma is the first vital step to be taken on the road to a full recovery - as my story will show you.

I want to continue to raise awareness of what was an endemic problem in the 1960s, and to give hope to others that by coming out of the shadows and into the light of the public eye, we can protect other children from the same abuse that thousands have already suffered in Catholic institutions around the world. The closed society of the past where those in authority were a law unto themselves, must never be allowed to happen again.

I also want to put on record that I do not wish to offend anyone – specifically decent folk who genuinely uphold the worthwhile values of the Catholic faith and do not harm others in doing so.

PART ONE

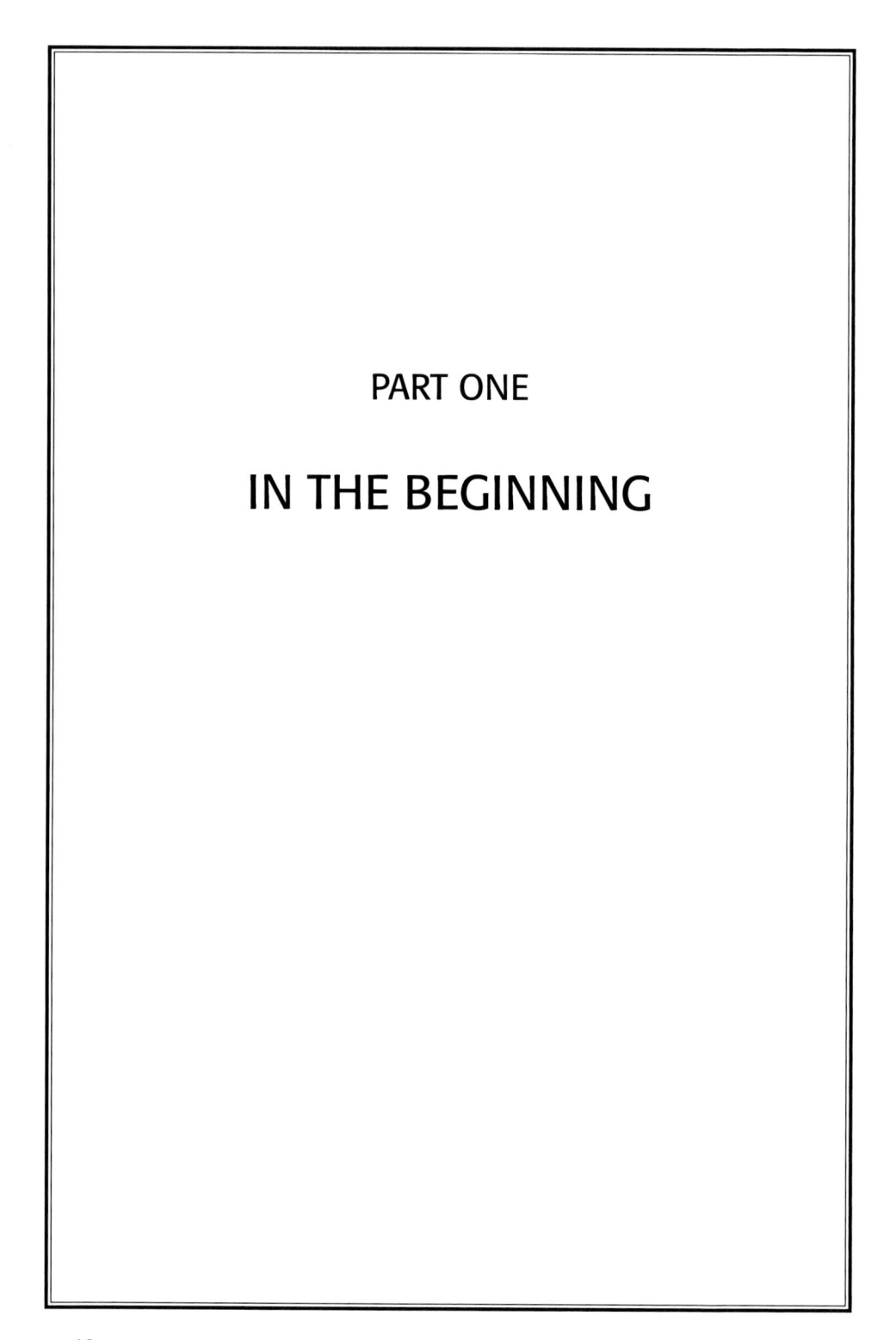

IN THE BEGINNING

'The Christian Brothers were fairly mangled fellows in Navan. Some speak highly of them, unfortunately I never saw that. I just remember the brutality, the straps that would fly out like viper's tongues, the beatings amidst the prayers – whack!'

Pierce Brosnan
(on his childhood education in Navan, Ireland.)

The year is 1961 and I am fourteen years old. I am at St Vincent's Catholic Approved Boarding School for Boys in Kent. Like all the other boys I was sent there for my care and protection and to gain an education. But it is a place of deepest misery and suffering.

In the communal showers one day I looked at my reflection in the full length mirror. The whole of my back was black and blue and dripping blood in places where the skin had been broken. Earlier that day I had been taken to a dormitory where my clothes had been ripped off by two Christian Brothers. Naked, my face pressed into the floor, I was flogged with a bamboo cane by Brother Arnold, a vicious and sadistic man with an explosive temper. During the beating he shouts and swears hysterically. The head teacher Brother De Montford, watches silently, relishing in my pain and suffering, my cries for mercy falling on his deaf ears. There is nowhere to hide and nowhere to run to. Under the hot shower later that day I think back to where it all began...

CHAPTER ONE
HAPPY DAYS ON THE FARM

'When I go into the countryside and see the sun and everything flowering, I say to myself, yes indeed all that belongs to me'.

Henry Rosseau

I was born to a poor but decent Catholic family in Norwich in 1947. I grew up on the Earlham council estate, one of those built to replace the rat-infested slums of post-war England. As a family, we upheld the values of the Catholic Church and enjoyed going to Mass and confession at Saint John's Church in the heart of the city on Sunday mornings. The church was a comfort to me. I liked the smell of the incense, the familiarity of the rituals and the sweet, soothing vibration of the hymns. The Parish Priest, Father Robert Manley, was kind to us and became a close family friend. He was to figure in my life right up until he passed away in 1983.

I was five when my sister Janet was born. When she was six months old, my father deserted us, returning to his home in County Cork in Ireland. My mother hadn't the courage or heart to tell me that he had left, and for three months I believed he was working away. She often said of Dad that we could have tolerated his drinking, swearing and gambling and his usual Irish jokes, but to never see him again was unbearable and heartbreaking.

The Church became even more of a comfort to her then as she struggled on, raising two small children alone. Her warm and constant serenity was testament to her faith which was never in question. Father Manley was constant and reliable in our times of need. He would turn up on his bicycle, balancing bread and potatoes in its giant basket at the front, knowing intuitively when my mother had no money to buy food for us.

We survived on public assistance after my father left. It was a period of austerity for many families in post-war England. In those days a household without a husband and father carried a stigma and was considered shameful. Despite this, we were a close-knit family and almost every day we would visit my maternal grandmother and aunts and uncles who lived about a mile away. They were also poor but we all supported each other through the hard times. From the time my father deserted us, I called myself David Armstrong, rather than use his name.

As a small child I attended the local infant school, which was a cheerful place. The teachers were kind and I recall my time there with fondness. In 1953 the children were all given a Commemoration Book and a tin of toffees in celebration of the Queen's Coronation – we made them last for months. The streets on the estate where I lived and the nearby woods and fields were our playground, and we loved to rummage in the bombed out buildings of the city not far away.

At ages as young as eleven, a few of the boys from our estate would work Saturdays on the cattle market in the city or pick fruit on the local farms. Sundays would be spent at Earlham Park, with its rolling grassland that led down to the river. In hot weather we would paddle in the shallow waters and splash about having fun. We had some wonderful days out and I cherish the memories.

At nine years old at school I met and made a lifelong friend – George, the son of a farmer Bob Ramsbottom. I was welcomed into the Ramsbottom family as one of their own. The whole family worked hard on their hundred acre farm, milking the cattle herd and harvesting crops of potatoes, carrots and swedes. It was located a few miles away close to the village of Bawburgh.

Bob Ramsbottom was a plump, jolly soul. He had a ruddy and weather-beaten face and was always smiling despite having more than a few teeth missing. Rain or shine he always wore a mackintosh, battered hat and

Wellington boots and smoked a briar pipe of sweet smelling nosegay tobacco. His presence in my life filled the huge gap my father had left and I felt I belonged there. He knew of the hardships my family had suffered, of my father's drinking and gambling followed by his desertion and my mother's struggle to make ends meet. I told him that I would like to be a farmer one day like him. He said it would be hard work, but smiled and said I should give it a try.

He gave me small jobs to do such as cleaning out the cowshed. Mrs Ramsbottom taught me how to milk the heavy cows that lumbered in from the meadows every afternoon. Eventually, by the age of eleven, I was working on the farm every weekend. I rode the tractor into the fields and hoed and raked in vegetables and throughout the seasons I gathered in the soft fruits, often eating as many as I had gathered.

The Ramsbottoms provided me with everything a farm worker needed; a pair of men's leather work boots and an old rain mackintosh once belonging to George's older brother. Suitably kitted out, I worked out in the fields in all weathers.

Sometimes a cow would break loose and we would chase it down the narrow country lane waving a stick at it, shouting and laughing, eventually capturing it and returning the poor beast to the herd. Life was good for me. The work was hard but I loved every minute.

By 1960, when I was thirteen, I was working not only every weekend on the farm, but also two full days during the week as well when I should have been attending school. I was beginning to grow physically strong but could barely read or write. At the age of eleven I had moved to Saint Thomas Moore's Catholic School in the city, also known as Heigham House. I detested going there; in hindsight I felt that the teaching standard was poor. My memories of the place are limited to learning the Lord's Prayer, being marched regularly in columns to services at the nearby Roman Catholic Cathedral, and queuing silently with the other children waiting for the daily caning. As a result I attended school less and less.

From my earnings on the farm I saved enough money to buy a second-hand bicycle to get me to work and back. At first my mother wasn't aware that I worked on the farm during the week when I should have been at school. I would leave the house in the mornings dressed in my school uniform but would cycle up to the farm instead and then change into my farm working clothes.

She soon found out, however, where I was spending my days and begged me to go to school. I would relent for a couple of weeks and go, but I disliked the school routine intensely. I felt guilty for deceiving my mother but the classroom could not compete with my love of the Norfolk countryside and working with nature in the fields. I think Father Manley understood this and when my bicycle was stolen he helped me to replace it. It's funny but in all the years I knew him he never once talked about religion with me, or with any of his other parishoners I suspect. He probably realised that our earthly needs heavily outweighed our heavenly ones.

Bob Ramsbottom was pleased with the cheap labour and during the summer months I would work every day from dawn until dusk. The farmhands taught me how to handle a gun and poach for pheasants at night.

Because I was the youngest, the other farm hands were protective of me and made a fuss of me at Christmas time, buying presents for my family and me. I would often be invited to have breakfast or Sunday lunch at their homes.

At the end of a long, hard day working in the fields with the beautiful heavy Suffolk Punch horses, we would sit at the edge of a field drinking cold tea from a bottle and eating the last sandwich of the day, tired but contented, satisfied with our day's work. Life was simple and good back then and I didn't have a care in the world.

CHAPTER TWO
ARRESTED AGED THIRTEEN, 1960

'After careful consideration it had been decided to send me to a Catholic Approved Boarding School.'

Very early one bright, sunny morning in July 1960, with the dew gently evaporating and the dawn chorus of birdsong filling the country air, I felt glad to be alive. I had awoken at five a.m sharp in my home at 21 Stevenson Road on the outskirts of Norwich and my first thoughts were of Mr. Ramsbottom, the farmer.

The only thing in my thirteen year-old mind at that moment was to get to the farm as soon as possible to assist him with his duties, milking the cows and cleaning out the barns. But something was about to happen that would initiate the ending of my happy days working in the beautiful Norfolk countryside and trigger a whole series of traumatic events over which I would have very little control.

After cycling the few miles to the farm by my usual route I found Mr Ramsbottom had already started the milking. He gave me a hot cup of tea and a bacon sandwich as was his habit, and after tucking into these, I settled down happily into my usual routine as his assistant.

Later in the morning he asked me to help 'clear out' some wood pigeons and rats which had been making a nuisance of themselves eating his crops. At about eleven clock, inside fields adjacent to some hedgerows flanking nearby cottages, I aimed the shotgun and let off a couple of shots to fell some pigeons.

A housekeeper came out of one of the cottges and asked what I was up to. I explained that I was clearing vermin under Mr. Ramsbottom's orders and she smiled and said: 'Carry on, you're doing a good job.'

I moved off along the lane and continued the work. About half hour later after I had finished, I was walking back along the lane which led to the farm, when a village policeman appeared by chance, riding along the lane towards me on his bike. He stopped and asked me what I was up to and I explained as best I could .

He then said he would have to report me for being in possession of a gun, under age and without a licence. I told him I had not misused the gun and I didn't know a licence was needed. He asked me if I realised how dangerous a shotgun could be near a public highway, then confiscated the twelve-bore and took my name and address and home details.

Because I was afraid of getting Mr Ramsbottom into trouble, I said nothing about the fact that I was working under his instructions and I did not tell the farmer about my encounter with the policeman either. The shotguns were kept in the barn at the farmyard and I just acted afterwards as if I had returned the twelve-bore to its place among the other guns.

The next Sunday morning a police car arrived at my council house home and my mother was very upset by this. We saw neighbours looking out of the windows at us. I was cautioned and the police took a written and signed statement from me. I accepted full responsibility for my actions, and later an official summons was issued for me to appear at the Norwich Juvenile Court in the Guildhall in the centre of the city.

My first experience of crossing the law was very frightening and although I felt I had done nothing wrong, I was fearful of the consequences. My mother was shocked at the news that I would have to attend a court hearing, but naively we hoped and prayed that my innocence would prevail.

A week later at Norwich Juvenile Court it was decided that a social enquiry report was necessary before my punishment was decided. I was remanded on bail whilst this was arranged. Three weeks later I was summoned to the Guildhall Court in the centre of Norwich. Father Manley accompanied me that day.

I arrived in a nonchalant mood believing I would receive a warning and be home in time for lunch. I waited in the grand hallway until I was called into the courtroom where I was asked to stand in front of a long wooden table where the three magistrates sat – a man and two women. The charges were read out along with a statement of my circumstances; that I had no father at home and hardly ever attended school. Father Manley spoke on my behalf. I then had to wait outside while a decision was made.

About twenty minutes later I was called back into the courtroom. The lady juror delivered the verdict, saying that after careful consideration it had been decided to send me to a Catholic approved boarding school. Today such places I believe, are called "community homes". I was told that this was not a punishment but for my care and protection and so that I could gain an education and learn a trade. I was to be taken there straightaway and not permitted to return home to my family to say goodbye to my mother and sister.

Father Manley supported the decision and believed that I would gain an education at this school that would benefit my future. However, I wasn't convinced that I liked the idea at all. Once outside the courtroom he reassured me that I would be well cared for at the school. He told me not to worry and that he would tell my family of the court's decision. I had never been away from home before and it was difficult not to get upset; but I tried to put on a brave face.

An hour later I was travelling in the back of a police car to Bramerton Lodge, a remand home in Norfolk. There I was to wait for a placement at an approved boarding school. Bramerton Lodge was five miles from the city centre. It was a beautiful period house with extensive grounds and it housed about twenty boys and ten girls. The Chief Officer in charge was a kind and friendly Glaswegian, the rest of the workforce were school teachers and I always found them to be friendly and helpful.

My days were spent in the classroom, and in the evenings we watched a black and white television. Our favourite programme was a detective series called 'Dragnet'. When we weren't watching television we would sit in the lounge and talk to each other. When all the outer doors were locked up at night, we were sent to the dormitories. Some of the older boys would risk life and limb climbing out of the windows and across the roof to the girl's dormitory, but being a somewhat shy "country boy" I never did.

On the first Saturday there, my mother, grandmother and sister came to visit. They were upset with the outcome but hoped I would not be away too long. I found it really difficult to hold back the tears when it was time for them to leave. Little did I realise at this time that during the following months, events would occur that would be life-changing and I would never be the same person as I was then.

CHAPTER THREE
SAINT VINCENT'S

*'I was like a lamb to the slaughter…
darkness started to seep into my heart.'*

A week later I was told that I would be going to St Vincent's Catholic Approved School in Dartford, Kent and the following day was taken there by car by a kind social worker.

It was a warm summer day and I remember enjoying the passing scenery during the ninety-mile journey. It was the furthest I had ever travelled. Before that any travelling had been limited to a twenty-mile day trip to Great Yarmouth for a day at the seaside.

St Vincent's Catholic School was built in 1875 and became an approved school for a hundred and twenty boys in 1933. It was run by the Presentation Brothers, a branch of the church founded in 1802. On initiation, the Brothers took three promises – poverty, chastity and obedience – and usually lived together in communities. The expressed mission of the Presentation Brothers was to 'form Christ in the Young' and to achieve this through education. The Presentation Brothers worked with a wide range of ministries assisting the homeless, elderly, disadvantaged youth and the Romanu people. During my time there they dressed in black cassocks, the same regalia as priests.

We arrived at about midday and I remember then feeling slightly anxious. But from this time onwards, it would be like entering into hell, tying my stomach in knots and almost paralysing me with fear. We drove through the open black iron gates and pulled up at a pair of large wooden doors. At the sound of the bell, a Brother came to the door and led us across an immaculate hallway and into the office of the head master, Brother De Montford O'Sullivan, who spoke to me from behind a large wooden desk.

He was tall and thin, his black hair was scraped and combed back. His nose and chin were long and sharply angled, his thin lips hardly visible as they pressed together in a hard line. Despite his unsmiling face, my first impressions were that he was quite friendly. He chatted in a broad Irish accent to the social worker about our journey and made some small talk with me. Then the social worker handed over some papers to the Brother, wished me the best of luck and left.

I looked around the room at the many religious paintings and statues. They reminded me of Sunday church attendance that I used to enjoy back at home and I felt I would be safe here. My knowledge of the Christian Brothers was that they referred to themselves as 'married to God'; and to me and the outside world they were perceived as kind, caring and law-abiding people who put the welfare of others before themselves. I had no reason to doubt this then but in hindsight, I was like a lamb to the slaughter.

Brother Demontford politely enquired of my family and said he hoped I would soon settle in. He explained the school's routine to me and made it clear that any acts of disobedience would not be tolerated. This seemed quite usual and didn't really perturb me.

The Brother who had been quietly watching during the introduction and briefing told me to follow him along a corridor to the clothes store where I swapped my clothes for the school uniform; a shirt and pullover with short trousers and army style black boots, which felt about three sizes too big. We then walked along another corridor and into a very long room with wooden benches along each side.

While we walked I asked the Brother if I could wear long trousers. I explained to him that I didn't like short ones because I didn't feel comfortable in them. Without any warning, I received a hard slap across the face and he shouted at me, telling me to take what I was given and calling me "an ungrateful little bastard".

The blow was hard and painful and I found it very hard not to cry. I had worked long hard hours on a farm often doing a man's heavy work but I was a softy at heart and this unprovoked attack frightened me. Dazed and confused I kept quiet, and we carried on walking to the locker room where I was allocated a locker in which to keep my few possessions. In the matron's office I was given a plastic toilet bag, toothpowder and brush. The matron, with her soft voice, seemed like an angel to me after the harshness of the Brother who had just hit me. I began to feel very homesick for my mother and grandmother.

I was then left to my own devices, so I went to the dining room where I met some of the other boys. At the table I told them about the slap I had just been given. One of them said that I was lucky that it had not been 'Nutty Arnold', referring to a Brother who was apparently notorious for his ruthless brutality to children. If it had been him I would have got a 'real beating', I was told. He had acquired the nickname because of his wild and vicious temper. Later on during my stay at St Vincent's I would often be on the receiving end of this man's violence. I was soon to learn that he merely pretended to be a normal human being.

* * * * *

From the time of my arrival, I made the decision that I would settle down and behave well so that I could return home as soon as possible. I really enjoyed the company of the other boys and discovered that I loved to play football with them in the big school yard; and I played whenever I could.

I became familiar with the school's routine. We attended Mass every morning at 7 a.m. and then after breakfast the day would be a series of whistles blown to herd us into lines to go to the classrooms or workshops for the older boys.

At four-thirty we would all line up for the communal showers. I learned to keep my wits about me after witnessing one of the Brothers who regularly towelled down some of the boys, paying special attention to their genitals. I always told him I could manage when asked if I needed help getting dry. One of the other boys laughed as he warned me not to bend down in front of him as he was known as "a right old queer". I didn't see the funny side, so from then on I would often go without a shower when that particular Brother was on shower duty.

It quickly became clear to me in fact, that the Brothers were sadistic and cruel and ruled the children with an iron fist. They used their control to intimidate and frighten us, especially the smaller or younger ones. But even the older, stronger boys knew they had no chance against a group of grown men.

It sickened me to see the other boys in there, their backs black and blue where they had fallen victim to one of the regular floggings in the dormitories. During the lunch hour, if we stood at the bottom of the stairs, we could hear them screaming as they were being beaten.

Some of the facilities at the school were excellent, particularly for sport. A variety of training courses was also available in the workshops, but after the daily beatings it was difficult to aspire to anything. Fear and misery, I soon found, was widespread.

Not all the staff were Christian Brothers; some were ordinary civilians who would take us to the local cinema on Saturday afternoons. In contrast they treated us decently and we knew from things they said that they disagreed with the Brothers' maniacal behaviour, which as far as we were aware, went completely unchallenged. They most likely feared for their jobs.

The cooks, gardeners and handymen also seemed like decent people to me, just simply earning a living there. I felt that if *they* had managed and run the school it would have been a good and happy place to be and may have achieved the objectives of the Presentation Brothers' mission statement. We always looked forward to the outings with them and we left our fears behind for a short time.

* * * * *

I had been at the school for about a month and apart from the first slap on the day of my arrival, had managed to avoid further conflict. Then one night I woke up in bed to find that my pyjamas had been pulled down and a Brother was sitting on my bed in his underwear fondling me. I reacted by shouting loudly at him to stop and he fled from the room. In the dim light I could just make out his face. It haunted me for the rest of the night and I lay awake worried and frightened to go back to sleep.

I scanned my memory searching for something I might have said or done that could have encouraged this event, but I could not recall having ever seen this Brother before. Despite this I felt I had somehow been responsible for his attention to me. Guilt started to shadow my sense of reason and darkness started to seep into my heart.

The following morning I was still thinking about what had taken place the previous night and was getting increasingly nervous about seeing the Brother who had abused me. I scanned the yard uneasily to see if I could see him, but he was nowhere to be seen. I found out later that he was an administration worker in the offices and was approaching his retirement. Occasionally I caught a glimpse of him carrying an armful of papers, and it was a huge relief when I realised that I would not have to see him every day.

After a while, we learned which Brothers to avoid, but I tried in fact to avoid them all, even those who were quiet and never bothered us. The only time I ever spoke to any of them was in the classroom when they were teaching and then I would only answer if spoken to.

After Mass on Sunday mornings we had to clean and polish the school floors and dust the nooks and crannies until the place was spotless. In the afternoons we would play football on the sports field. We looked forward to the evenings when, after tea, the Brothers would hand over to the civilian staff.

There was also a hierarchy among the boys based on who was the toughest. I found my own ways of getting along with them and gained their respect through playing competitive sport, or simply by being friendly and getting on with everyone whenever possible. A group of these older and tougher boys controlled the flow of cigarettes and tobacco into the school and I became their runner along with a boy called Mac.

Mac was a big sturdy boy with a ruddy complexion and thick red hair. He had been in a children's home before he came to the school. During the lunch hour, our task was to scramble through a hole in the perimeter fence and run to the local shop to buy the stock and then run back undetected. We would receive a packet of cigarettes for our efforts. Luckily we were never caught.

One lunchtime, a Brother I vaguely knew by sight, approached me and told me he wanted to speak to me. He told me to follow him across the yard and up some stairs to a small isolation room on the second floor near the dormitories. Internally I panicked; thoughts were rushing through my mind that something awful had happened at home and I was about to receive some bad news. Once inside the room, he locked the door and I panicked even more, sensing something much more sinister was about to happen to me.

My heart pounded in my chest. He ordered me to take off my clothes. Embarrassed, I refused but he then slapped me with an incredible ferocity and pushed me against the wall. He cupped his hand around my throat and squeezed it. He told me to do as I was told.

I was absolutely terrified and through my tears and sobs said: 'Yes Brother.'

Once undressed, he told me to lie on the bed. Then he stood over me, raised his cassock and masturbated himself, never once taking his eyes off my naked body. When he had finished he said: 'Now that wasn't so bad was it?'

He then told me to get dressed and go about my business. In a state of fear and confusion I went back to the yard and sat on the ground with my back to the red brick wall, shaking and sobbing. One of my friends asked what was wrong, but I was ashamed and unable to repeat what had just happened to me. Instead I told him I wasn't feeling well.

That night, too frightened to go to the dormitory and not sure what I was doing, I left the school grounds, blindly following an instinct to get away from the place where the horror of the abuse had occurred the night before. I wandered through the streets not knowing where to go.

The streets of Dartford were unfamiliar to me and the place felt just as hostile as the school did. I spoke to no-one and walked the streets until I was exhausted and the night had turned cold and dark. I turned into an alley at the end of a neat suburban street and found a garden shed to sleep in.

Alone in the shed that smelled of creosote and damp wood, I didn't feel any safer. I tried to sleep, but thoughts scrambled around my head all night, searching for a solution, a plan of escape, a respite from the fear. For comfort I thought about my family, especially my mother. The tears fell and I sobbed myself to sleep exhausted.

I woke early, disoriented and fearful of being found by someone. Back to school was the only place I could go and I retraced my steps until I found the school, feeling a stab of fear in my stomach as I approached the gates. Dirty and tear stained, I walked through the hallway and into Brother De Montford's office. He didn't appear surprised to see me and told me without emotion that the police had been informed of my absence and that he would now inform them of my safe return. He did not appear to be angry and told me to go and have some breakfast. Relieved, I made my way to the dining hall and believed that would be the end of it.

* * * * *

Later that afternoon as I finished up my lessons in the classroom, I was approached by two Brothers who told me to follow them across the yard and up the stairs to the dormitory. I was trembling with fear and anticipation; by now I knew what to expect.

Once inside the room I saw Brother Arnold swinging a bamboo cane; his face was a mask of cold rage. Standing beside him next to the window was the head, Brother De Montford, clearly enraged too. Using foul language and shouting, he told me he would not tolerate any disobedience especially from boys who absconded.

I was told to undress and put on a pair of shorts but I totally froze and was unable to move. I had always been shy by nature and had never been comfortable undressing in front of anyone, including my own mother, so the idea of taking off my clothes in front of these monsters was pure mental torture and the events of the day before were still all too fresh in my mind.

I begged and pleaded to be let go but my pleas were ignored. The four men ripped my clothes off until I was naked and held me face down on the cold stone floor. I screamed in agony as the cane smashed across my back about twenty times. When I was finally released I ran across the room crashing into lockers and beds; my back burned and felt as though it was on fire.

* * * * *

That night in the communal showers looking in the mirror I could see the whole of my back was black and blue and dripped blood where the skin had been broken. I couldn't stand under the stream of the shower, the pain was too unbearable. I stood shivering in the corner, fighting back tears but unable to look anyone in the eye for the shame of what had clearly happened to me. I felt someone watching me and turned to see a new boy who had arrived only yesterday. He was staring at my back, the dried blood and swollen bruises. He reminded me then of the boy I used to be, when I arrived.

I learned later that this new boy had been sent from a children's home. He was incredibly pale and thin, and his limbs were frail and weak looking. I invited him to play football several times but he preferred to sit with his back to the red brick wall in the yard, lost in his own world.

His bed was four down from mine in the dorm. One night I woke to see his blankets had been pulled back and a Brother was sat on the edge of the bed dressed only in his underpants. I watched helplessly as he moved closer and put his arms around the boy. Immediately a rage rose up inside me and overcame the fear of reprisal. I shouted loudly at the Brother and called him "a dirty sick bastard", and he backed quickly out of the dormitory, protesting his innocence.

* * * * *

After playing football during the lunch hour one day, a group of us sat on the ground chatting and the conversation turned to the subject of girls. One of the younger boys called 'Shrimp', because of his small size, told us he was learning how to have sex. We asked him if he had secretly been with a girl and he replied that he had not, but that one of the Brothers had been taking him upstairs to the isolation room and teaching him.

I'm sure I wasn't the only boy among us that day who wished for the courage and strength of a grown man in order to confront the Brother responsible and punish him for this heinous crime against an innocent little boy. But we were only boys and we knew we wouldn't stand a chance against them. I would meet Shrimp again some years later when both of us had become men. By then he had become a highly disturbed and violent rapist, who was locked up for the safety of humanity.

* * * * *

Father Manley had answered my weekly letters from the time I had arrived and now wrote with news that he was coming to visit in the first week in November. I was very happy with the thought of seeing him and I reflected on how such a good man could be part of such an organisation. His role in my life had always been more of a family friend than that of a priest and I trusted him implicitly. I thought about the vow of celibacy he had taken and how this would deprive him of a loving relationship and raising children of his own. I felt Father Manley would have been a good father and husband. I painfully recalled my own father's irresponsible behaviour and eventual desertion, and the injustice of it all simmered inside me.

Visits were held in the dining room on a Saturday afternoon. It was quiet that day because most of the boys had been taken to the cinema. Father Manley was sitting at a table as I entered the room and when he smiled and shook my hand I could see he was searching my face for clues as to how I was feeling.

At first the conversation was light; he talked of his visit to my family and of how much they missed me. But all were well, he said which was of paramount importance to me. I tried to be brave and hide the truth, but as we talked I found it almost impossible to hold back the tears. I could not find the courage or words to describe the events I had suffered in detail, but I told him that the Brothers in charge at St Vincent's were brutal and their behaviour often maniacal.

He listened quietly. I knew that he cared and we talked for about an hour. Before leaving he told me never to feel guilty about what was happening or to blame myself. He said he would hope and pray that the place would not change me into a person I was not.

Watching him leave, and left alone in the empty dining room, my thoughts were of home, my mother, my friends on the housing estate and Duke, my black Labrador who had been my constant companion on the farm. I'd had him since he was a small puppy, a birthday gift from the farmer Bob Ramsbottom. I visualised their faces in my mind and imagined myself back there with them. The image brought momentary joy and I savoured the feeling for as long as I could, my eyes squeezed tightly shut…then a bell rang and a Brother's voice boomed at me to move and the familiar sensation of fear and resentment returned once more.

CHAPTER FOUR
CHRISTMAS AT HOME

*'I trained my mind to select only the
thoughts that would give me joy.'*

For some weeks after Father Manley had visited, I noticed that the Brothers' attitude towards me had softened a little - but I still kept out of their way as much as possible.

At Christmas time I was allowed home for a week. The night before the home leave began, I tossed and turned all night and my stomach fluttered with every thought of leaving and seeing my family and home again. Finally I woke at dawn and leapt out of bed to get dressed and wait for the time I could leave. I had received letters from them every week but had not seen them for nearly five months. It had seemed like a lifetime.

I travelled by rail across London to Liverpool Street Station. During the two-hour train journey to Norwich the oppression and humiliation of the past few months started to lift as I grew accustomed to life outside the school. Whenever my mind wandered back to the abuse, I quickly pushed the thoughts away and buried them. I wanted only to think of the normality of home and the people who loved me, and I trained my mind to select only the thoughts that would give me joy.

Although it was bitterly cold I decided to walk the three and a half miles home from the station, making the most of the freedom to walk familiar streets. I walked into the city where the annual Christmas fun fair was in full swing. The generators resounded around the old city walls and the fairground lights flashed manically. Children screamed with delight on the merry-go-round and the sweet sticky smell of candy floss and toffee apples made my mouth water. I realised I had been missing out on so much these past months.

I walked amongst the brightly coloured stalls in the market place and bought some roasted chestnuts and a cup of tea with the small amount of pocket money I had received at the school. The hell of the past few months ebbed away as I warmed my hands on the cup of tea and ate the chestnuts as I slowly ambled home.

Arriving at my home, I fought back tears as I hugged and kissed my mother and grandmother. My mother marvelled at how much taller I had grown and my sister threw herself at me when she arrived home later that evening, hugging me and crying. She told me tearfully that she really missed having me around the house.

The Christmas tree twinkled in the corner of the front room and familiar decorations hung down from the walls and over the mantelpiece where a fire glowed. We spent the evening sitting close to each other in front of the fire catching up with all the local news. I never once mentioned the school or what was happening to me there throughout the entire leave, and I was careful not to undress in front of them in case they saw the scars and bruises from the floggings. I didn't want to talk about it. It would be many years in the future before I was able to do so.

* * * * *

Christmas Day celebrations were held at the home of my grandmother Nanny Armstrong and it was full of relatives. Finances had improved lately because my mother had found a part time job and my aunts and uncles were now working, most of them in the armed forces. My youngest uncle had joined the Navy but was on home leave to be with the family for the festive season. We exchanged gifts, took photos of each other and played the usual board games and listened to the radio. We did not have a television at the time but we were a happy family group who enjoyed each other's company.

One of my uncles had bought an old black car from one of his army friends and I spent much of the home leave riding around the city with him, both of us hoping it would not break down. A boy who lived nearby had managed to acquire an old ex-army motorcycle and he and I would push it along the road and take turns riding it across the local fields or through the woods. I spent the last two days of my leave doing this and having a great time.

CHAPTER FIVE

BACK TO HELL

'We have become accustomed to the religious lie that surrounds us. We do not notice the atrocity, stupidity, cruelty with which the teaching of the Church is permeated.'
Leo Tolstoy

When it was time to return to St Vincent's I just couldn't bring myself to go back. Nobody but me knew the nature of the punishment that would be handed out for late returns, so my family allowed me to stay until the police inevitably arrived – which they did three days later. I wrenched myself from my family's goodbye embraces and was taken back to the school in a police car.

That first night I was locked in the isolation room where I had previously been abused. The next morning I was taken to the dormitory where I was flogged with a stick. I tried not to scream throughout the ordeal but it was impossible. Aside from the brutality of the beating, the humiliation of having to stand in a room skinny and naked in front of four grown men who were out of control, was more than I could stand. It was a week before the pain subsided enough to play football.

In 1961 when I became fourteen, life at the school continued as normal but the differences in my emotional condition were beginning to surface. I felt very angry with the Brothers and found it almost impossible to hide these feelings. More than once I foolishly tried standing up to them.

On one occasion a teacher called Brother Michael had slapped me hard across the face because I had sworn at him. I fell backwards from the blow and smashed my head on a steel window frame. I spent three days in the infirmary having my head stitched up and suffering from double vision. I don't remember any inquiry into the 'accident'. On many occasions I told the Brothers what I thought of their cruelty and was always beaten almost senseless for my trouble.

I spent all my free time playing football in the yard in all weathers. For the next few weeks after my fourteenth birthday, life at the school carried on as normal with the sound of boys screaming coming from the dormitories at all hours while being beaten for the smallest offence against discipline.

* * * * *

One day a packet of cigarettes appeared in my plastic toilet bag – and then every second or third day another packet would arrive. I didn't know who had put them there, it was a complete mystery to me. I asked my friend Big Mac if he knew anything but he was just as mystified.

Big Mac – real name Barry – was from Kings Lynn, a Norfolk country boy like me, tall and stocky. Big Mac had been an enthusiastic amateur boxer back in his hometown. His huge arms and shoulders bulged beneath his shirts and he walked with an exaggerated swagger. He feared no one, so it seemed. He had been sent to St Vincent's for not attending school - and for his aggressive behaviour when he did.

His thick, wiry, ginger hair was interrupted by a fairly large and permanent bald patch over his right ear, resulting from his nervous habit of tearing out strands of his own hair. If this habit or bald patch was ever mentioned by one of the boys he would be rewarded with a black eye – he could be a bit of a bully with some of them. Luckily I had a knack for getting along with him and Big Mac and I became good friends.

I asked him one time if the Brothers had ever abused him because I had often wondered why certain boys were picked on more than others. I was surprised when his face turned bright red with embarrassment and he stammered as he told me of a time when a Brother had appeared beside his bed one night. But that before anything could happen, he had squared up to him and told him to piss off.

He also confided that shortly after his arrival he had been flogged in the dormitory by Brother Arnold and a couple of others. After the flogging he was unable to control his temper and had punched one of them sending him crashing to the floor. He told them that if they ever touched him again he would kill the lot of the sick bastards. I remember thinking that this must have been an effective tactic because I never saw any of the Brothers bother Big Mac.

* * * * *

One afternoon it was my turn to clean the Chapel. I was obediently polishing the floor when Brother Michael entered. He called me over to the vestry and I thought maybe he wanted me to clean it. Once inside the room, he closed the door and came up really close.

He asked me if I'd got the cigarettes OK. Now I knew where they had come from! I didn't answer. His face was too close. His breath stank of stale coffee. He said: 'Don't be shy. Can I touch you?'

He reached down with his hand and felt between my legs. 'You have nothing to be frightened of', he said and started to squeeze with his hand.

Time stood still and my limbs felt like lead. Although not as big or physically strong as a boy like Big Mac, I eventually found a strength I had not known before and managed to push him off me, calling him a filthy bastard.

Shocked, he backed out of the chapel; but locking eyes with me, he said quietly: 'You will not beat us, boy!'

On the way back to the dorm I punched a wall to let off some steam. I was raging with myself for not pushing him off me sooner. I felt a sickening shame. Why hadn't my arms and legs moved more quickly? That night, whilst trying to sleep, the sensation of his hands on my body replayed in an endless loop in my head that revolted and enraged me at the same time. I was terrified of what might happen when he found me again.

I saw him several times over the next few days and he made a point of making eye contact with me. My discomfort and embarrassment was evident. I looked away, but not before catching his mocking and twisted smile; he was also smacking his lips as if feeding on my fear.

* * * * *

The many incidents of physical and sexual abuse were beginning to weigh me down. A burning hatred for authority was growing inside me like a cancer. My earlier tactics of burying the memories and replacing them with happy thoughts of my family and home life was just not working for me any more. Repressing my reactions of guilt and injustice had created an internal vat of molten rage. In short – I was going crazy.

Mentally and emotionally the incidents of abuse were too numerous to deal with and when they weren't happening to me they were happening to some other boy while we were forced to listen or watch helplessly as the abuse stormed on. I recognised a sense of evil was all around me and it was permeating my thoughts and actions. It sapped my will to be kind and loving, like the boy I used to be. That boy was completely lost.

* * * * *

Everything that happened during this part of my life would fester on inside me and cause deep psychological problems in the future. From this time onwards I had no contact with the Brothers and if they came in my direction I would walk the opposite way. I was on my guard at all times and there were few people in my world that I could really trust. Big Mac was probably the only one.

I had become best buddies with him. We shared cigarettes and sweets and gave each other moral support when we were down. The Brothers' brutality was common knowledge at the school but I never, ever mentioned the predatory sexual behaviour of the men in conversation with my fellow pupils. I could not bring myself talk about it with anyone.

The men who ran this school had no empathy whatsoever for the needs, welfare and safety of growing children. The feeling of being imprisoned went beyond being unable to leave; we were also captive to the religious teachings, unable to express our own opinions or speak freely.

As an example of this oppression, one particular Brother had a nasty habit of forcing a boy to stand on the sill of an open window. Then, if he spoke out of turn, the boy would be pushed out of the window and onto the ground below. It is a miracle there were not more serious injuries than there were.

After one such incident a boy said loudly so everyone could hear, 'It's a good thing we are on the ground floor.'

The Brother replied with a twisted smile, 'I did not know that we were.'

It is a blessing for our families that they never knew at the time what was really going on in there.

* * * * *

During the following months I avoided the Brothers like the plague. I occupied my time playing football whenever I could. The brutalising and sexual abuse in the dormitories continued, and it became normal and expected. I didn't realise that this period would affect the rest of my life forever, as children never do. And I'm not able even now to describe every incident that took place.

Many grey crosses, discoloured with the passage of time, lay neglected and forgotten in the adjoining cemetery, the resting place of former pupils who had died in the past from illness. Probably orphaned or abandoned and therefore denied a burial in their hometowns, these boys lived and died in the care of these men who were monsters to them; and they probably died deeply unhappy and unloved. It is only thanks to a modern and open society and the power of the news media that such neglect of human responsibility is now exposed and will hopefully be eliminated.

* * * * *

Easter was a period of near hysteria at the school. The chapel was cleaned from top to bottom and filled with fresh flowers and an endless queue of boys filed in and out for confession. A bishop came to conduct Mass in Latin.

To us boys and probably most of the Brothers it was indecipherable and meaningless gibberish. Afterwards we had to file past the altar and kiss the ring of the Bishop's gloved hand. Forced into this act of hypocrisy, I found myself remembering a Brother's recently spoken words: 'You boys are nothing but vermin.'

Yet here in the chapel the same man would be on his knees showing respect to a wooden cross or plastic statue.

CHAPTER SIX
ABUSE WITHOUT BOUNDARIES

'Once inside the chapel, I was made to remove my shirt and was told to stand in front of the altar with my arms out to the sides to form the shape of a cross...'

Twisted Catholic morals formed the basis for many a classroom lecture at the school. One morning soon after Easter, the Brother taking our class warned us against the temptation of the carnal pleasures that he himself, a supposedly celibate man, was denied. He tried to teach us that we must avoid the lustful demands of the opposite sex and that sexual intercourse with women was a filthy act.

I sat through the lesson willing myself not to tell the Brother how very wrong this all seemed to me. I wanted to scream out that it was normal for men and women to be together and it was the Catholic Church who had twisted the rules that in turn had twisted the minds of the Brothers. As I walked out of the classroom at the end of the lesson, I was unable to contain myself any longer and I told the Brother that I hated the Catholic Church and wanted to change my religion. Astonished, the Brother asked me in his thick Irish accent if I had meant what I'd said, and I replied that I had.

That evening I was made to pay for my outburst. Three Brothers came to me in the corridor and told me to follow them to the chapel where the mass had been held. One of them carried a long wooden stave similar to the ones I have seen used in mediaeval jousting. I could barely breathe as I followed them down the corridors and into the chapel. Once inside,

I was made to remove my shirt and was told to stand in front of the altar with my arms out to the sides to form the shape of a cross. I looked up and could see directly above me a large carved wooden crucifix that hung from the ceiling, my image replicated in its shadow.

One Brother stood in front of me, one behind, and the other to one side next to a statue of the Virgin Mary holding the child Jesus in her arms. I felt the stave smash against my bare back about six times – the pain was horrific and unbearable with each stroke. I screamed out in agony over and over again. Following what seemed like an eternity, the beating finally stopped and I collapsed to the floor. Quickly I was forced back onto my feet to be asked by one of the abusers, 'Are you sorry for insulting our beloved church?'

Loathing myself for my weakness I whispered through the pain, 'Yes Brother.'

I was then forced back down on to my knees and had to repeat that I believed in God the Father Almighty, Creator of Heaven and Earth; the forgiveness of sins; in Holy Mary mother of God and in the Holy Catholic Church. As I limped back to the dorms, I found myself feeling grateful because on this occasion I had only had to take my shirt off and not strip totally naked as with previous beatings.

Nevertheless I was unable to join my friends on the football playing field for many days and I wished again for a way out of this hell-hole and an end to the madness. I didn't know it at the time but my wish was about to be granted, sooner than I had hoped for, albeit under the most bizarre circumstances.

And this was the last time I was to see Brother Arnold's twisted face or walk through the gates of St Vincent's, home and hell to me, for one whole year.

PART TWO

OUT OF CONTROL

'A repressed memory is like a noisy intruder being thrown out of a concert hall, you can throw him out but he will bang on the door and continue to disturb the concert. The analyst opens the door and says if you promise to behave yourself you can come back in.'

Theodore Reik, Psychoanalyst.

The remainder of my teens and the first few years of my twenties should have been the best of my life. The stiff upper lip of Britain was about to be softened by Beatlemania, mini-skirts and LSD. Whilst the boys that I grew up with were starting apprenticeships, dating girls and daring to grow their hair long, my life took a very different turn.

St Vincent's had set the tone for the next few years that followed; violence, abuse and near madness. Only this time, it was me who was going mad.

In just six years, the repression of the abuse I suffered manifested a raging and bitter young man, severely misunderstood because I could not bring myself to talk about why I was so angry.

A Catholic upbringing in the 1950s had ensured I knew of no way to freely express my emotions. In addition to that conditioned repression, I am a very private man by nature and did not share my private business with anyone else. However, the rage found its way out via a release valve more times than I care to recall. Several detonations later and I find myself locked up in Britain's most notorious mental institution that detained the most disturbed and dangerous criminals in Britain. How did I end up there?

CHAPTER SEVEN

SENT TO PRISON AGED FOURTEEN

'I am a Norfolk man and glory in being so.'
Horatio Nelson.

In August 1961 I was granted summer leave from Saint Vincent's – a two week reprieve from the madness that was becoming normal to me. It was a relief to be back home and I played out on the streets with the children I had grown up with until the sun went down every night. For the first week my sister and I picked fruit at a local farm with some of our neighbours. The summer was in full swing and it was good to earn some money while the sun shone down on us.

For most of the second week I spent my time swimming in the local river with the boys from the Earlham estate. We used to dive off the railway bridge and into the murky water, climbing out to line up on the bank and bask in the hot sun for a while before diving in again to cool down. Around dusk we would return home as red as lobsters. These were happy days.

I never returned to the farm, my emotions were too mixed up on the subject. The memories I have of working in the fields without a care in the world were, and are, the best of my life, but at that time they came with the burden of guilt that I carried for deceiving my family and not going to school.

As always with the home leave, the time flew past all too quickly. When the day for me to return arrived, I told my family I could not face it again.

They allowed me to stay at home until the police arrived, still not aware of the kind of punishment that awaited any boy who was late returning to an approved school.

I enjoyed another week of blissful family life before the police eventually turned up. I was taken to the police station to wait for transportation back to the school. I waited in the office and watched the detectives go about their work, typing up their reports with one finger on clunky black typewriters.

I chatted with one of them, who I noticed later went on to become a chief superintendent, and spoke to him of my fear of returning to St Vincent's. He looked thoughtful for a moment and told me he may be able to help me out.

He left the room and returned four or five minutes later. He sat down next to me and asked if I would be interested in doing a deal. I asked him to explain what he meant. He said that there had been a number of theft and damage offences committed in Norwich, for which the culprits had not been found or charged. He went on to suggest that if I admitted in court that I had committed these offences that it would delay my return to St Vincent's and they would get their books cleared up – regardless of whether or not I was innocent.

As crazy as this sounds, it seemed like a good deal to me at the time and the policeman reassured me that it was a good solution all round. The consequences of admitting my non-existent guilt for these crimes were only explained in terms of the one thing that would *not* happen – going back to St Vincent's. And that the more charges I admitted to, the better the prospects for not being returned there. That was all I wanted to hear!

I agreed to the deal and spent that night in the police station cells. The following morning I was taken to Norwich Juvenile Court where I pleaded guilty to one charge and had another ten offences taken into consideration. I was remanded to prison for reports and to await sentence.

CHAPTER EIGHT
LIFE IN PRISON

'I know not whether laws be right or whether laws be wrong. All that we know who lie in gaol is that the wall is strong and that each day is like a year. A year who's days are long.'
Oscar Wilde

I was taken to Norwich Prison in a police car and presented to the reception wing for new-arrival processing. Once my details had been taken down, I was made to take a bath in about three inches of water. I dressed in the prison uniform of grey trousers, blue and white shirt and heavy black shoes.

I picked up my blanket roll, plastic chamber pot, white pillow case, tooth brush and shaving gear and was told to follow a warder along a long corridor. All the gates were unlocked and locked behind me as we walked to the main four-storey high cell block. A steel wire net separated the ground floor from those above it.

My allocated cell contained a single iron bed and a wooden corner toilet unit. As the door was locked behind me, a tremor of panic ran through me. A prison rulebook hung from a nail on the wall, I took it down, sat down on the hard iron bed and read through it.

At four-thirty I could hear doors being unlocked and the booming voices of men, their footsteps rumbling as they climbed the steel stairway and walked along the slate landing back to their cells after a day in the workshops. My cell door was opened and I joined the file of men queuing at the food hotplates, collecting my meal on a steel tray. That day we had beef goulash with bread and butter and tea in a plastic mug.

Speaking to no-one I carried my tray back to the cell. Shortly after that the door slammed shut. Alone with my thoughts, I wondered what other teenagers would be doing at this time of the evening. Then I wondered what the children at St Vincent's would be doing right now. I looked around me and although unfamiliar and frightening I felt safer than I had done for a long time. There were no Christian Brothers here.

The door opened so I could put my empty tray out for collection and my plastic mug was filled with cocoa at the same time. Then it was 'bang-up' until the next morning. It had been a long day and I wasted no time in falling asleep.

The next morning, I was given a brief health check by the medical officer before being sent to see the governor in his office. I was given a date for my next court appearance and issued a job with the cleaning team along with some of the other new younger arrivals.

I soon became used to the routine: cells were opened up at seven thirty a.m. to slop out and wash. Then after breakfast at nine o'clock, we exercised for half an hour in the yard, walking in anti-clockwise circles. We worked until midday then after lunch more walking in circles, then back to work until four-thirty p.m. The ground floor had rows of tables and chairs where some of the older men and under-twenty-ones could eat, and it was also used as a place for socialising known as the 'Association' Area'.

In the evenings we played darts or board games or would sit and chat in the Association Area. Lock up was at eight p.m. Cleaning was an easy job – we weren't bothered by anyone and left to get on with it. If we finished our work early, we could get a cup of tea from the kitchen and sit around in each other's cells, chatting or playing cards for matchsticks.

The warders were not unkind and went about their jobs as they should. I felt that whatever my fate was to be for admitting to the offences, that I had made the right decision and had finally escaped St Vincent's and the reign of the Christian Brothers. This place felt like a sanctuary in comparison, even for a boy of fourteen surrounded by hardened criminals.

Listening to the men talk and sensing the attitude of the warders, it became clear that sex offenders, paedophiles or 'nonces' as they were referred to, were not tolerated by society, either inside or outside the prison walls. In prisons, nonces were segregated under 'Rule 43', which protected their vulnerability to attacks from other prisoners, such was the common revulsion for their crimes. Learning this validated my own loathing for them as an undisclosed victim, but at the same time it began to fuel an internal rage.

Whilst cleaning a long corridor one afternoon with one of the other young prisoners, we noticed two green sliding doors which were locked. We had never seen them opened and asked one of the passing warders what lay behind them. He told us that the doors led to the 'topping shed' another name for the gallows. Next to it was the 'condemned cell'.

I told him I was curious to know more, so the next day he borrowed the key to this disused area and showed us around. I stood in the small cell where men had waited to die. I tried to imagine how they had felt, knowing they would walk to their deaths at the end of the hangman's rope. It spooked me for days.

* * * * *

This was a local prison and most of the men were from the Norwich area, there to serve short sentences for various petty offences. There were vagrants, who I learned would throw a brick through a police station window in the hope of getting locked up; bad debtors who were sent to prison for being unable to pay off their debts which were later written off, leaving the bill for their incarceration to be picked up by the tax payer. Then there were the old lags, basically serving life sentences in instalments. To them prison was home.

Whilst on remand here, a probation officer visited me to prepare a social enquiry report in preparation for the court hearing. These reports provide background information about the offender and were necessary in order for the court to decide how to deal with my case. I was shown to an interview room and the probation officer started the interview by asking me how I had arrived at this situation. I found myself telling him of the misery I had endured at St Vincent's.

I did not talk of the sexual abuse but spoke of the brutality and the unyielding regime that did not care for children or help rebuild their futures. The probation officer wrote down everything I told him on the report.

On my way out of the interview room I walked past the governor's office and couldn't help noticing a man in his late sixties who was singing and dancing, clearly full of joy. Because it was an odd sight in this kind of place, I stopped and asked him why he was so happy. He said he had just been given five years imprisonment – it turned out he had only just been released a month earlier after serving a seven-year sentence. He had spent the whole of his life behind bars. At an early age he had become locked into a subculture where prison felt more normal than civilian life and he continually re-offended just so he could return to the place where he felt 'safe'.

* * * * *

The month on remand passed without incident. I returned to court where my mother and grandmother met me and were allowed inside the courtroom with me. I stood in front of three female magistrates who looked sternly down on me. I pleaded guilty to the offences that I had not committed, as agreed with the police officer. Nobody mentioned the fact I had been at the Approved School in Dartford at the time of the offences and because I had pleaded guilty, no further evidence was requested by the magistrates or prosecuting officer.

The prosecuting solicitor explained to the court why I was there and read out the offences to which I had pleaded guilty. Then the social enquiry report was read out and the magistrates listened without expression while they heard about some of the mistreatment I had received at St Vincent's. Finally I was asked if there was anything I wanted to say before the decision was made and a verdict on my future was given.

For the next twenty minutes I verified the social enquiry report to the magistrates and told them that the past year at St Vincent's had been a living hell for me. Again I could not and did not talk of the sexual abuse but I explained once more that the regime at the school had been brutal in its treatment of children. They listened intently to what I had to say. I noticed their stern expressions soften a little. I told them that if I was given a chance that I would lead an honest and decent life. We were then told to wait outside.

The forty minutes spent waiting for the judgment seemed endless. Back in the courtroom, the spokeswoman said that they had listened to all I had to say and wanted to know if I had really meant my promises to not get into any more trouble, if given a second chance.

I told them that I had meant every word. She then went on to say that they had considered the situation very carefully and had determined that I had suffered enough. So I was being given the chance I had asked for, and would be placed on probation for one year.

The tension of the last few hours finally broke and I cried in my mother's arms. The relief at not having to go back to St Vincent's was overwhelming. I felt I had been granted a new life.

* * * * *

Instead of returning to live with my mother I went to live with Nanny Armstrong, my grandmother, because my family believed that my young aunts and uncles who lived with her would have a steadying influence on me, particularly Uncle John, who despite being sixteen years older, had always been more like a brother to me. I had been raised in a Catholic environment but my grandmother and her children took the faith to a new level. Mass was attended every week and the local priest was a regular visitor to their home.

My own faith had remained constant and unwavering before my stint in Saint Vincent's. Before that I had never questioned the authority of the Church or had reason to mistrust the teaching of the Catholic religion. Indeed it had been a comfort to me as a child to sing at Mass and I had always looked forward to Father Manley's visits to the family home. I remember praying as a child and feeling the inner calm and comfort one attains from one's faith, an inner knowing that I was looked after, and that no harm would ever come to me while in God's presence. .

But things had changed. My association with the Catholic Church had been thoroughly tainted with cynicism during the year at Saint Vincent's and my faith had been thrown into question and lay hiding in a dark inner closet along with the secrets of my abuse.

After my release I returned home to a Catholic lifestyle with my family and a period of readjustment followed while I settled into a new routine. I started work at a shoe factory and did my best to keep my promise to the courts. But the disturbances to my emotional condition were becoming evident to me. I was withdrawn and didn't talk to anyone much, I trusted no-one and kept a tight lid on my emotions.

I still didn't divulge anything about the sexual abuse at Saint Vincent's. In those days there just wasn't the vocabulary to articulate such events and these things were rarely disussed.

Another subject I couldn't discuss was how to deal with my faith. Unarticulated, angry questions started to surface along with a feeling of betrayal. I thought long and hard about what God had done for me in my short life. Where was His protection when I was at St. Vincent's?

I asked myself what kind of God allowed his servants to abuse children, to beat them with a stave until they screamed and bled, to strip them of their clothes and humiliate them under the symbolism of the Cross?

One morning, instead of going into work, I found myself taking my questions and uncertainty to Saint John's, the church where I had attended Mass every week as a child with my mother and sister. The noise of the traffic fell silent as I walked up the steps and through the arched doorway at the west side of the building. I entered the church, passing the place where I had been baptised as a baby, and took a seat in a pew at the front of the church where I remained silently seated for the whole day.

I remember feeling very much alone that day, even desolate. I grieved for the child that used to sing here, clutching his mother's hand and putting his pocket money into the collection box. That child had been lost somewhere. I looked up at the large crucifix high above the altar and I prayed; 'Dear Lord help me, give me hope to go on! Show me the light – the way!'

But there was no light, only the light from the flickering candles on the altar. I held back the tears of helplessness and desperation. I found no answers there, only emptiness.

As I walked out of church into the cold night air, I knew that I would never return. The one answer that I did find that day was that God did not exist for me – all I'd ever had were the superstitions of an outdated and twisted religion which, far from saving me in my hour of need, had only delivered me to the devil's doorstep, vulnerable and trusting. By casting out my old beliefs I hoped that the past, too, would leave me. As I walked home I told myself that I could live a decent life without the 'help' from the Catholic Church. Tomorrow was another day and I would really try to do my best to live it well.

* * * * *

My job at the shoe factory was quite enjoyable, it was a sociable place, the people were cheerful and once a week I would go to the cinema with some of the crowd I worked with. Weekend mornings I would help out at a local riding stables outside Norwich, and in the afternoons when my work was done I would be allowed to ride the horses along the country lanes and in the fields. I saved up and bought a second-hand motor scooter. My family were really pleased that I was getting along normally, and everything was going so well. It looked as if my life was on the right track at last.

However, around nine months after my release, I started to suffer with terrifying panic attacks. Images of the abuse I had suffered, flashed back in the dead of night and I would not be able to sleep. I would lie awake most nights trying not to think about the violence and abuse, but the more I tried not to think about it, the more the thoughts pervaded my waking moments the next day.

With these memories, anger started to surface too. I could not bring myself to discuss the abuse with anyone, and in an attempt to block out the pain, I drank a lot of alcohol at weekends. But once I was drunk, all the anger would rise – and I would go crazy.

I did not realise at the time that I was emotionally and psychologically damaged. I found myself locked up at the local police station on many occasions following wild drinking binges where I would commit some kind of violent offence. My family did everything they could to keep me out of trouble and were really supportive. But I could not get the memories out of my head or talk about them. So round and round they went in my mind. The more I drank to try and erase them, the more they flourished.

One incident of abuse at St Vincent's stands out in my memory more than most, even to this day. At breakfast one morning, one of the boys came down to breakfast with a split lip and bruised face. His name was Mark. I really liked him, he was good-looking boy, a little like the singer Billy Fury.

He was always happy and not a trouble maker. Mark told me that Brother Arnold had beaten him and immediately I felt outraged on his behalf. It seemed so unfair and I couldn't shake off the feeling of injustice – I wanted to hurt Brother Arnold back.

I spoke of my need for revenge for this sadistic and unprovoked attack to some of the other boys, but they reminded me why he was nicknamed "Nutter Arnold" and tried to talk me out of it. But I couldn't let it go.

A few days later while playing table tennis in the games room, I challenged Brother Arnold as he walked past me – asked how he could do such a thing to my friend. Without emotion he responded by pulling his huge fist back and punching me hard in the face before walking on. I still find it hard, even today, to comprehend how a religious man could behave in such a sadistic way to a child.

* * * * *

In the winter of 1964 at the age of seventeen, my behaviour suddenly spiralled downhill. I stopped going to work and was prescribed tranquilisers and other medication to calm my nerves and help me sleep at night. My days were spent hanging out in coffee bars with low-life people who were also unemployed, living in bedsits and taking illegal drugs. We scrounged benefits from the social security and used our hand-outs to get high or drunk. My family tried, but it seemed there was nothing anyone could do to turn my life around.

Taking drugs and drinking alcohol was a way of calming my nerves, which were shot to pieces by this point. My efforts to make something of my life were overshadowed by feelings of worthlessness and self-loathing. My confidence had been chipped away during my time at St Vincent's, but instead of it returning to me on my release, the problem became progressively worse.

By the summer of that year I was extremely unstable – accumulating many convictions for drink related offences. I was lucky and was given many chances by the courts to turn my life around, but when a person takes the road to self-destruction, it is very difficult to turn back.

In August of that year things came to a head. I was sentenced to two years imprisonment to be spent at a Borstal for an assault on a policeman and criminal damage to a public house. A Borstal was a type of youth prison run by the Prison Service, intended to reform seriously delinquent young people less than twenty-three years of age. Today they are I think called 'Youth Offender Institutions'.

After three weeks spent in Norwich prison I was transferred to Wormwood Scrubs Borstal wing. I was to be held here whilst I was allocated to another prison. The place was dirty, smelly and overcrowded and after a month of being locked up for almost twenty-four hours a day, seven days a week – sharing with three others in a cell designed for one – I was extremely happy to leave. Myself and a few other boys were picked up by a coach and taken to HMP Wellingborough in Northamptonshire.

Security Borstal HMP Wellingborough was a new purpose-built prison for the under twenty-threes, built on rough farmland in the

Northamptonshire countryside. During my stay, working gangs of boys would landscape the farmland into gardens. My first month was spent in an Induction Block where we all struggled with the military-style regimes of marching in the yard and meticulous bed making. We were then moved over to one of the two main blocks. The cells were small but comfortable and lock up was at nine o'clock.

We would be made to rise each morning at seven o'clock to run around the yard in shorts and army boots. After breakfast we went off to our different jobs – I worked in the gardens. We worked standard hours with an hour for lunch. After six o'clock was 'free time'. We could watch TV, play table tennis or go to the gym. I preferred the latter – I enjoyed keeping myself fit. Weekend mornings were spent cleaning our cells, ready to be inspected by the governor. In the afternoons we played football on the sports fields. A film was shown in the gymnasium on the occasional Sunday afternoon.

After six months of this repetition I became bored with the whole situation and, as the Borstal prison was only a couple of years old, I decided to achieve notoriety and be the first prisoner to escape. I hatched a plan with some others. This involved making a distraction for the guards so that I could make my escape. Our plan was to swing into action as we finished work on Friday evening. Whilst still outside, one of the boys would fall to the ground pretending to be sick and the other boys would gather around him, causing the guards to focus their attention on the commotion.

Meanwhile, I would run in the opposite direction towards the high steel wire fences, climb up them and throw my jacket over the barbed wire to enable me to roll over it and climb down to the ground below. Then all I had to do was run to a six-foot high wall, climb over that, then a six-foot high perimeter fence – and then into fields of freedom.

I had been training in the gym every night, so was very fit. When the time came to execute the plan, to our amazement everything went as intended. I felt absolutely euphoric as my feet touched the ground outside of the perimeter fence and I ran as fast as my legs would carry me across a ploughed field. Once over that, I was just crossing a road when two screws in a car spotted me and gave chase.

After climbing the high fences wearing heavy working boots I was totally exhausted but the adrenalin was flowing and I just kept running. The two screws finally caught up with me but with the adrenalin still pumping, I decided to fight them. I managed to wrestle one of them to the ground and threw a punch at the other one – at which point I was overpowered and taken straight back to the punishment block. I got a good beating that night, they did not take kindly to teenagers assaulting Borstal officers. They preferred it the other way round.

The following morning I was presented to the governor. My actions of the previous night were considered worthy of a few weeks at Reading Borstal Punishment Centre – and this institution would prove to be another where the men who ran it were a law unto themselves.

As I awaited transportation to Reading, anticipating further punishment, I wondered what had happened to the good Catholic boy who had loved working on a farm, who had helped milk the dairy herd at dawn, and happily fed the farm animals and horses that he loved to ride. Here in his place was a psychologically damaged teenager filled with guilt and anger, full of hate.

CHAPTER NINE
CRACK-UP

'The warders with their shoes of felt, crept by each padlocked door, and peeped and saw with eyes of awe, grey figures on the floor; and wondered why men knelt to pray, who never prayed before.'
Oscar Wilde

HM Prison in Reading, now used as a present-day Borstal Centre, was a typical example of Victorian prison architecture. Based on a design used for HM Pentonville, the accommodation blocks were shaped into a cruciform. The prison was originally designed to carry out what was the very latest penal technique of the time, known as the separate system. It also served as the site for local executions. Oscar Wilde was famously imprisoned there from 1896 to 1897. It closed as jail in 1920 and was used as an internment site during both World Wars. When I arrived in 1965, it was one of the toughest Borstal training centres in the country.

The first thing I learned at Reading was that punishments were always doubled up. Talking with other inmates was not allowed, and we were permitted to talk only when spoken to by those in authority. We worked for six hours a day and had two hours hard circuit training. Lock-up was from five-thirty pm until seven o'clock the next morning.

In the evenings, the warders would creep along the landings and peep into the cells. They turned the key silently in the lock, then three or four of them would charge into the cell and throw vicious punches at the unsuspecting cell resident. All too much I was reminded of the Christian

Brothers, because like them, these men made up their own rules. Their behaviour would reinforce an already present hatred for authority.

Some teenagers arrived at Reading as lambs and left as lions, others the reverse. After two months of endless hours banged up, I had not been permitted to talk to anyone and the brutal regime was starting to make me feel crazy. I had never been a hard or tough guy, but steadily my reactions to these daily injustices – the abuse of power – began to pathologically affect my emotive state, transmuting fear into pure rage, which I regularly directed at those in charge. The rage numbed me, I felt I could not be hurt anymore. There was nothing left inside except the hatred for authority and I sought to release it at any opportunity.

One summer's day in the workshop, cutting layers of rubber from copper cables, we sweltered in the rising temperatures. We were made to wear ties and our tunics had to be buttoned up to the neck and we were not permitted to loosen them. A skinny young lad working next to me complained and was punched in the head about twenty times by Patterson, the merciless workshop warder.

We all watched helplessly, pitying the poor lad; we had all been there. Inside I felt the pressure building up and I sought a release. I provoked Patterson by whispering something to the kid in full view.

Patterson came at me, ready to take a swing at my head. At that second a red mist came down and the pressure inside me detonated – and I totally lost all control. I leapt out of my seat and punched him with all my strength. He staggered backwards and squealed like a pig; my punch had landed well. I watched all this as in slow motion, the reality of the situation quickly starting to sink in, and I backed off, sensing through my rage the consequences of any further action. They would half kill me for sure.

The alarm bell was activated and very quickly half a dozen of the heavy mob arrived. I was dragged into the main building by a group of them and violently assaulted, then thrown naked into a cell in the punishment wing. This was to be a truly unforgettable experience.

The windowless cell was roughly 6 feet square with double steel doors. It felt like I had been buried alive in a large steel coffin. I immediately felt panicked and breathless, there didn't seem to be enough air to breathe normally. Above me was a small observation window through which the screws would look, day and night, jeering at my suffering. Solitary confinement means exactly that – I saw no one during my stint in there. Meals were pushed in on a plastic plate and the doors quickly slammed shut. I endured three weeks of it – each day drove me a little closer to insanity.

When back on the main wing in my usual cell, I learned that the governor had added another month to my stay. Every day for the next few weeks I was brutally attacked by the screws, and spent the last two weeks of my stint there in the hospital wing because of the injuries.

I returned to Wellingborough Prison still with a broken shoulder which was treated and fixed at Northampton General Hospital. It would be a reminder of the sick people who ran Reading prison. The punishment there was supposed to break people into total submission, but for some like me it had the reverse effect.

As soon as my shoulder was healed I was a raging bull and caused as much mayhem as possible. I had spent a lot of time locked up alone with my memories of St Vincent's and was feeling senseless with anger most of the time. I spent many days and nights in the punishment block for offences against discipline.

My fellow inmates quickly noticed the change in me since my return. My moods were explosive and uncontrollable. I blew a fuse at the slightest provocation or irritation. The only time I settled down and behaved was when the governor threatened to send me back to Reading. One broken shoulder was bad enough, I did not want another one. I was eventually released in March 1966 aged nineteen, after serving twenty months.

CHAPTER TEN

BACK HOME

*'...I had found it impossible to form lasting relationships.
I carried a burden of guilt; the sexual abuse from
St Vincent's had taken something from me.'*

On my release I returned once more to the home of my grandmother. My aunts had now married and my uncles were in the Army or Navy. My sister was doing well at school and my mother was engaged to a good man that she had known for a number of years. They would later marry and spend the rest of their lives together. As always, it was a relief to be home again amongst loving family and living in a safe environment.

My nerves were in a bad way and I was still taking prescribed medication to help calm me. I tried to lead a normal life and went to work in a flour mill which stood on the banks of the River Wensum. I filled sacks with flour from a giant hopper and loaded them onto a lorry. It was hard and back breaking work but I was earning an honest living and a free man. I hoped that the routine of normality would rub off onto my psychological condition.

Many boys of my age had steady girlfriends and were planning to marry and have a family but I had found it impossible to form lasting relationships. I carried a burden of guilt; the sexual abuse from St Vincent's had taken something from me. I didn't understand at the time but in hindsight I saw that the guilt and the buried shame sabotaged any relationships I tried to form. For the next few months, at least outwardly, it appeared that I lead a relatively normal life. As a family at weekends we would take ourselves off to Great Yarmouth or Lowestoft for the day and I have fond memories of those times.

As before, whenever I was released, I suffered with nightmares and memories of the past. Now of age, I found solace in alcohol, but it fuelled my rage like petrol poured on a fire. History repeated itself and during that year I was locked up in police cells on many occasions for drink related offences, such as criminal damage, getting drunk or trying to demolish a pub. I was a regular visitor at the Magistrate's Court and the only reason I was not sent to prison again was because I worked hard and the magistrates believed there was hope for me.

At this stage in my life I was beginning to believe that it would be possible to put the past behind me and live a decent life. But this was not to be. In December of that year, at the works Christmas party, I got very drunk and as usual all the anger surfaced. I left the party at about midnight and while walking home through the city centre I saw a copper. Seeing the uniform was like a red rag to a bull; my rage spilled over and I attacked him.

The town was busy that night with other drunken party revellers and they too began to get involved. Very quickly the fight turned into a street brawl which ended with lots of drunken men running down the street while the copper chased us, calling for back-up on his radio. Before too long a police van arrived and I found myself cornered in a shop doorway by a snarling police dog. The other brawlers had disappeared and managed to get away.

The following morning after a night in the police cells, I received a six-month prison sentence, suspended for a year. This meant that if I got into trouble during that period the prison sentence would come into effect and back I would go.

*Where it all began... St. John's Cathlic Cathedral, Norwich, where author
David Armstrong was baptised in the autumn of 1947.*

Where all the trouble began... the Norfolk lane today, where David Armstrong was stopped by a policeman while shooting vermin for a farmer in the summer of 1960.

David, today outside 21 Stevenson Road, Earlham Estate, Norwich, where he was born...

...another view of Stevenson Road today.

Author's sister Janet at home, aged five.

Constance, mother of the author, photographed at a party in Norwich with visiting Irish relatives of her husband Sean Hammond.

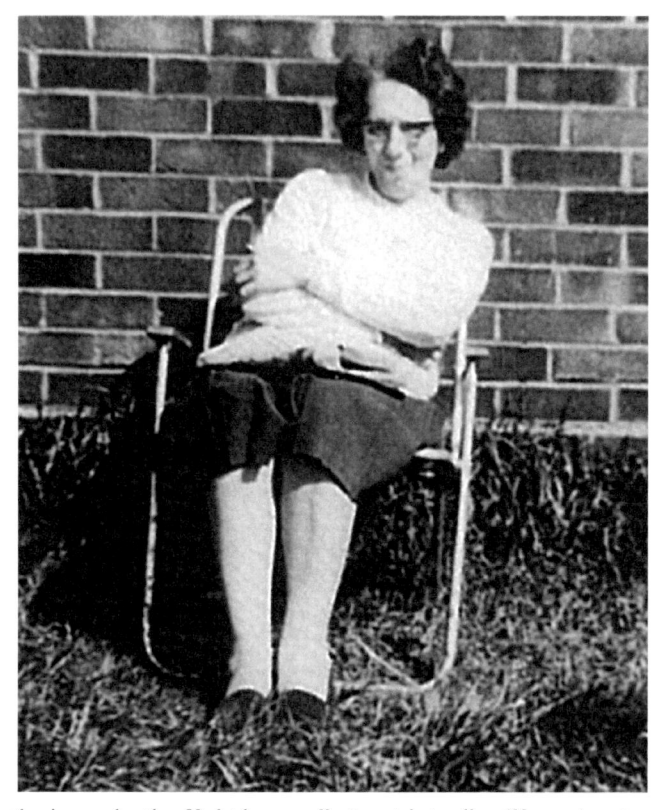

Author's grandmother Violet known affectionately to all as 'Nanny Armstrong'.

The author with his nephew Peter.

The author in 1985 with his sister Janet at her wedding.

St Vincent's which had been founded in 1876, closed in 1982, like several other similar institutions. The entire site, amounting to about 25 acres, excepting one acre for a new Catholic church, presbytery and car park, was sold to a developer. That individual razed all the buildings to the ground and built a new housing estate there. A little cemetery at the corner of the field, where staff and boys were buried from 1876 onwards, was excavated and the interred bones transferred to a new communal grave near the new church.

73

The author's uncle, Peter, in full dress army uniform.

The author (left) with his uncle John Armstrong in 1972.

The old Gate Lodge at Broadmoor Hospital.

Jimmy Savile pictured with Prime Minister Margaret Thatcher

*The author photographed in Eaton Park, Norwich,
just after his release from Broadmore in 1970.*

The author in 2014 at the Norfolk farm, near Bawburgh, where he worked happily for serveral years when a young boy in the late 1950's.

David, pictured with his uncle John Armstrong outside the farm.

The pomp and grandeur of St Pater's Basilica in Rome.

CHAPTER ELEVEN
BACK TO PRISON

'Physically and psychologically, I was in meltdown.'

Although I was still heavily into taking drugs and forever being locked up in police cells for drunken rampages, I managed to continue working and my family were still doing everything in their power to keep me out of trouble. But my state of mind was disturbed and I sensed that something had to happen. 'It' happened in August 1967.

I had got incredibly drunk in the local pub and was smashing the place up with reckless abandon. Several policemen arrived and I punched one of them a few times. Three weeks later at Norwich Crown Court I was sentenced to a year in prison for the assault and with the suspended sentence in effect, that made it eighteen months. During the hearing I called the judge a bastard and anything else I could think of and was bundled out of the court by half a dozen coppers.

I knew from the moment I went through the gates of Norwich prison that I would not be able to cope with a prison environment again. On the very first day of the sentence I was brawling with prison officers in the exercise yard and when the alarm bell was activated to summon the heavy mob, I stood my ground throwing fire buckets at them and anything else I could lay my hands on. Eventually I was overpowered and dragged into one of the punishment cells and given a good working over by the screws. The following day the prison governor awarded me a month in solitary confinement. Apart from half an hour of exercise in the morning and afternoon it was bang-up twenty-four-seven.

After that month banged up in solitary I was returned to a normal cell. I was feeling really sick because I had not eaten properly for a month and had only managed about two hours sleep each night. Physically and psychologically, I was in meltdown. I regularly threw things around in the cell making quite a noise. Once, out of total frustration I smashed my fist against the wall and fractured my wrist. The medical officer arranged for me to be taken to the Norfolk and Norwich hospital with a suspected broken hand.

After treating my hand, the doctor at the hospital noted my mental state. At that point he said I was gibbering and my eyes were glazed. He stated in his report that I needed psychiatric treatment but as there were no facilities at the prison for people with mental health issues – except to prescribe tranquilising drugs – it was recommended that I be seen at a local psychiatric hospital as an outpatient under escort. The prison governor overturned this recommendation, returned me to solitary, and the depression and anxiety continued along with the symptoms of being unable to sleep, eat or remain calm for a reasonable period of time.

Maybe the prison authorities believed that solitary confinement would help prisoners with problems like mine by teaching them a lesson, but it had the reverse effect on me. At the end of the confinement month I was switched back to the normal prison routine, but lasted only a week before the rage reared its fiery head again. It happened after a day in the workshop sewing mailbags all day. I picked up a heavy chair and smashed it into the door of the governor's office, breaking it open. Once inside the room I smashed out all the windows. Luckily he was not there at the time. I don't like to think about what could have happened if he was.

For the next few months my behaviour and reactive trigger to authority became increasingly volatile and I would smash up cells or go on the rampage. Once I climbed onto the roof of a cellblock, and on another occasion I had just collected my meal from the hotplate and on the way back to my cell I encountered one of the screws – renowned for being a bully – at the bottom of the steel staircase. As I walked by, he goaded me by saying, 'Have a good night, don't get drunk now…'

Being in a state of total depression there was only one way I knew how to react; I smashed him with the steel food tray and when the alarm bell was activated and screws came from all directions, I went ballistic throwing tables and chairs in their direction.

I quickly gained an audience and dozens of other prisoners goaded me on shouting, 'Go on Dave, kill the bastards!'

However, I needed little encouragement. The following day after a night behind double steel doors in the punishment block and a good kicking by the screws, instead of going in front of the governor to be punished I was placed in a hospital cell to contain me.

There was one kind warder at that prison. Most nights he would come to my cell and sit and chat for half an hour. He showed me pictures of his family and I would talk about my life back home. He genuinely wanted to help me. He would always bring along a paperback book for me to read or bar of chocolate. Five years later he left the prison service and we met up by chance in a snooker hall. We are still friends today.

* * * * *

In April 1968, not long after my twenty-first birthday, I had lost all remission and still had a few months left to serve. I could hardly get through a day without an incident of conflict or violence. I was skinny and pale, had barely eaten anything or been able to sleep for months. I was continually drugged into oblivion and banged up twenty-four-seven. I was a mess. Then another trip to the medical centre and finally I was interviewed by a psychiatrist. I'm not sure what was in his report but a week later I was told I would be transferred to a psychiatric hospital.

I left the prison in a taxi, handcuffed and squashed between two burly prison officers. I was heavily drugged and can't remember too much about the journey. I believed I was being sent to a local hospital that I knew of in Norwich – Hellesdon Psychiatric. I had a vague idea that it had to be better than prison.

I fell asleep for a while and when I awoke I saw that we were travelling south out of Norfolk. I asked the warders where I was headed and was told it was Broadmoor. Even in my drugged state the word sent shockwaves of dread through me. I then learned I had been sectioned under the mental health act, which theoretically meant that I could be detained for life alongside murderers, paedophiles and rapists. With a sense of impending doom I remembered the 'Topping Shed' and Hangman's rope that had spooked me at Norwich prison while on remand at fourteen years of age. I understood how those men must have felt. The rest of the journey was spent in silence.

What I could not have possibly foreseen was that this turn of events was to be the catalyst for much needed treatment and help that would eventually get my life back on track.

CHAPTER TWELVE
OFF TO THE CUCKOO'S NEST

'I must be a crazy to be in a loony bin like this.'
McMurphy, a character from the film *One Flew Over The Cuckoo's Nest*.

Broadmoor is a high security psychiatric hospital at Crowthorne in Berkshire. It opened as a mental institution in 1863 and has since become synonymous with some of Britain's most notorious criminals. It was the first custom built lunatic asylum in the world. At that time there was no precedent for an establishment having both medical and penal motives for its existence.

Many of the early inmates of that time were women who had killed their children while suffering from post-traumatic depression. Until 1948 it was a prison and then became a hospital which was transferred to the department of health, where its ethos was supposed to change inmates into patients.

The hospital, if I remember rightly when I was there, detained about 260 patients, most of whom had committed serious crimes such as rape, child molestation, arson and murder. There was also a minority group of men sent there because they were found to be highly disruptive at other prisons. I belonged in this group.

As I arrived, I thought that its high, imposing perimeter walls still gave the impression of a prison rather than a hospital. I was surprised at how stunningly beautiful the area was with the well kept lawns and pretty flower beds, and an avenue of lovely trees. Within these walls, red brick accommodation buildings blocks called "houses" sprawled out into the grounds. Each had its own walled garden called 'airing courts' that led down to the kitchen gardens, beyond which lay the extensive sports fields and a segregated female wing. It was a scene of outstanding beauty, a contrast to the ward blocks with steel bars at the windows, which housed men who had committed unspeakable crimes.

My first stop was the assessment wing. While I waited to be seen by the doctors, I watched men walking up and down the corridors staring into space and mumbling incoherently or talking to their invisible friend. I was relieved to notice a couple of young men that looked fairly normal, at least outwardly. They were dressed in civilian clothes watching television or playing cards or striking balls on a pool table. It was difficult not to think of the blood on their hands and the tragic circumstances that had brought them to an asylum. Regardless of the locked doors and high walls, I concluded quite quickly that this place was nothing like a prison.

Several psychologists and psychiatrists interviewed me. I was assessed as having a personality disorder of a social nature that was probably the direct result of a childhood trauma. I asked how long I would have to stay in hospital, and what sort of treatment I would receive. They told me that this disorder could progress to a more psychological disorder, from sociopath to psychopath, but it was up to me whether or not I wanted to get well again.

They said that if I behaved well and kept calm then I would not be held there for long; but there was no magic pill that would do it for me. I was asked several times if I had suffered abuse as a child. I finally admitted that I had but couldn't bring myself to discuss it with them. The pain of the humiliation was still raw and the secrets were buried deep.

My first month was spent at the coincidentally named Norfolk House. I spent a few hours each day in the occupational therapy room there. It was usually uneventful, but during my first month a young man who had killed his father ran amok hitting anyone who got in his way with the sharp side of a wood saw. Fortunately no one was seriously hurt, but I got caught up in the mayhem and my head was cut from a glancing blow, which had to be stitched up.

Another patient I crossed paths with was Joe. He had long grey hair and a long grey beard. He suffered delusions and believed that he was God. He walked around the day-room, 'blessing' people, raising his arms in the air and speaking in a language no one understood. I was not in the mood for this nonsense one particular morning, so when it was my turn to be 'blessed' I told him to piss off, adding that I thought he was a fake.

He flew into a rage and stormed up and down the room ranting, insistent that he was 'the one and only true God'. He was quickly locked in a room until he had calmed down. When he was allowed back into the day room, he approached me straight away and told me calmly that he really was the one and only true God. To keep the peace I told him I believed him.

* * * * *

There were many such delusional characters at Broadmoor. During exercise periods I watched a man in his sixties, stripped to his waist, prancing around the yard shadow boxing. Apparently in his youth he was an aspiring middle-weight boxer. He said he was training for the next big fight. I asked him how long he had been training and he replied, 'Twenty-seven years.'

The most difficult people to cope with were the paranoid schizophrenics. Always convinced they were being talked about, it was impossible to have a conversation with anyone while they were in earshot. They could not be convinced otherwise and a fight would usually follow.

Exercise time was generous; we had two one-hour periods when we could play football or enjoy some fresh air and socialise with the other patients. After tea we could watch television or play pool. Ward patients like me were dressed in civilian clothes, giving the place an air of normality compared to the prisons I was used to. Lock-up was at nine p.m., when we had to put our day clothes into a wooden box outside the cell-like rooms and change into pyjamas.

* * * * *

The fresh air and exercise did me the world of good and I was feeling a little better by the end of the first month. Sitting at an open window one evening looking at the lawn below, I spotted Jimmy Savile talking with a group of people. He worked as entertainments manager for the hospital whilst I was there and was later appointed chairman of a task force set up to advise on the governing of Broadmoor. On this particular day he looked like he had just walked off the Top of the Pops set; he was dressed in a red and yellow tracksuit, his long blond hair flowing down his back. I shouted down to him, 'Hey Jimmy how come you get paid for your lunacy and we get locked up for ours?'

'Now that is a secret I cannot divulge!' he shouted back and he made that funny little noise he was famous for.

Inspired by him, I joined the entertainments committee and after that I would often see him and we would always chat about this and that. He talked a lot about his beloved mother who he called 'The Duchess'. Back then, taking him at face value, I always found him to be a kind and generous man. He actively supported many charities throughout his life.

At Broadmoor he would organise concerts in the central hall, often inviting famous pop groups, actors or solo singers to put on a show. In a place where virtues were scarce, Jimmy was a dependable figure who we respected, a sane and trusted friend.

* * * * *

At the end of my first month and induction period I was moved to Cornwall House – each of the six accommodation blocks were named after a county. The supervision on this ward was not so intense and was not for the very dangerous patients. However if we were not behaving ourselves we would be moved back to one of the other blocks where we were watched more closely and there were more staff on hand to cope with trouble.

There were a number of elderly people on this ward who sat in chairs staring into space for most of the day, lost in their own worlds. Others appeared to be normal if you were unaware of the terrible crimes they had committed.

On one occasion, I walked into the toilets to find a man just about to hang himself. On another I called for help when I found a man slashing his wrists down to the bone. Both were saved but I often wondered if I did them any favours.

I settled into the routine and after several months I was given a job in the new purpose-built workshop that manufactured shoes. Other than doors that locked behind us, it was like working in any small shoe factory. Weekends and evenings during the summer we would go to the sports field to play cricket or football.

Social evenings were held once a month in the central hall and we were permitted to sit and talk to the female patients for the evening. For the rest of that year I avoided trouble and kept my nose clean, making the best of the situation.

I was among a number of patients who were considered highly disruptive whilst serving sentences at other prisons and had been sent there to calm down. Some had famously rioted at Parkhurst Prison on the Isle of Wight. I felt I could make friends of these men because although they were aggressive and undoubtedly had a violent past, they were not the type to harm women or children.

Instinctively I wanted nothing to do with the paedophiles or rapists. My psychiatrist said that this was discriminating behaviour – I felt I was being judged for not wanting to talk to men who had carried out terrible crimes against innocent women and children. Little did they know that this was because I had once been such an innocent child.

CHAPTER THIRTEEN
BLOCK SIX DUNGEONS

'I would see the faces of the Brothers in my nightmares and relive the humiliations of naked beatings in the chapel.'

I befriended a patient, Roy 'Pretty Boy' Shaw, the boxer. He was known for his criminal activity in the underworld and was associated with the Kray twins. He was an incredibly strong, but quietly spoken man, with staring eyes. Metal weights were not allowed in the hospital so he used heavy bags of sand in his daily workout. We both loved to play football and keep fit, and through our love of sports we became good friends.

I got into an argument one day with a hard case from Newcastle called Freddy. He was always fighting and pushing people around, mostly those less able to defend themselves. During the argument he threatened to rip my head off at some point in the future. He was a huge man, with a menacing demeanour and I knew I would be unable to match him physically.

With Roy on the sports field a few days later, I mentioned his threat. A couple of days after that Freddy walked onto the ward with two shiny black eyes. He approached me rather humbly and apologised for threatening me. I then heard a rumour that he and Roy had had a fight. I asked Roy if it was true, but he just said, 'Nah' in his Cockney twang, 'I just gave him one good punch and threw him down a flight of stairs and luckily he survived.'

I heard that the day before I arrived at Broadmoor, Roy had broken the jaw of one of the screws. When I got to know him, I knew that this must have been a provoked attack, because he was generally good-natured and didn't look for trouble. If he took a pop at anyone it would be the bullies that deserved it. The staff were all terrified of him, which amused those that were fortunate enough to be on the right side of him. I counted myself as one of the fortunate few.

The first time I saw Roy lose his temper was on a Saturday watching football on TV in the dayroom. He was minding his own business when a huge, six foot six inches tall, tank of man walked past and said 'You don't look that tough.' Roy followed him into the toilets and jabbed him with his left hand as he stood at the urinal. The deluded fool fell to the floor with his dick in his hand, pissing all over himself. They became friends afterwards but both knew who the governor was. The day I left, Roy shook my hand and said, 'The trouble with this place is there's too many paperback gangsters.' Whatever that meant.

* * * * *

A few weeks after Christmas in 1969 I was transferred to Gloucester House where there was even more freedom for patients who had behaved well. We could even make our own meals in a small kitchen and the gates to the walled gardens were open all day. My spirits were raised slightly, but then without warning after a few weeks of being there, I became severely depressed and withdrawn, choosing not to talk to anyone unless it was absolutely necessary.

The psychotherapy was digging up events that were once again coming back to haunt me at night. I would see the faces of the Brothers in my nightmares and relive the humiliation of naked beatings in the chapel. One night in the dorm, things came to a head. I shared the dorm with ten other men, all murderers, rapists and paedophiles. At about nine-thirty p.m., half an hour before lights out, one of the men was talking openly about how he had murdered a young girl. He laughed as he recounted the story.

This touched a raw nerve so I got out of bed, walked over to him and punched him. I wasn't the only one offended by his lack of remorse.

Little Jimmy, a fearless Scot and a good friend of mine, jumped up from his bed and head-butted him. Soon the others were punching and kicking him and a brawl broke out which quickly turned into a dormitory riot, all ten of us violently fighting. The alarm bells were quickly sounded which was a good thing because by the time the warders arrived, we were throwing chairs and lockers at each other.

Three of us were taken over to 'Block Six Dungeons'– the segregation unit where prisoners were left to 'cool off'. Stripped of my clothes I was locked in an empty cell and given only a blanket where I was to be held for three weeks.

*****

I had sunk into the lowest depression I had ever known and felt that my life was absolutely hopeless. I didn't want to open my eyes or look at another human being. Consumed by self-pity and hatred for the world, I didn't want to live like this but was unable to help myself. I listened to the tortured and lunatic cries of the other patients in the block as they ranted all night and fought in the corridors whenever they were let out. With nothing but a blanket in a bare cell there was nothing to distract me from their cries, my own endless self-recrimination and a bitter hatred for my pathetic life.

Near the end of my stint in there Jimmy Savile came to see me. Framed in the doorway, his white hair flowing onto his shoulders, it seems absurd now in light of the recent revelations of his crimes against children, but at the time, deluded and drugged, I thought I was being visited by an angel.

He sat on the floor with me and we chatted about Norwich, his mum, the entertainments schedule – all sorts of things. He never ran out of things to talk about. He was wearing a lovely silk shirt and I told him how much I liked it. He promised I could have it if I settled down and behaved.

He asked me eventually to recite the Lord's Prayer with him. I refused and told him that I saw religion as hypocrisy, so he closed his eyes, bent his head and recited it alone.

Before he left the building he spoke to the male nurses. I don't know what he said to them, but later that day I was allowed to get dressed and go back up to the day room, a very unpleasant place. There, the number of attendants was doubled, and no-one was allowed to leave the room without permission. On the faces of many men was the look of vacant madness; some sat with their heads down, heavily sedated. When they got up to move they shuffled slowly as if manacled. Many had languished in this place for years with little hope of recovery from their damaged minds.

It was here that realisation of the hell I had found myself in finally hit home - and it hit hard. The first patient I encountered here was Shrimp, the small boy from St Vincent's who had been groomed and sexually abused continually by one of the Brothers. Not much bigger in size but now a dangerous and violent rapist, he spent each day sitting in a chair with his head slumped forward, drugged out of his head.

This would go on for about two months, after which he would be sent back to a ward with a normal routine. After a few weeks he would become incredibly violent and the cycle would start again. There were a few others on the wards whom I recognised from St Vincent's and many more from other Catholic Schools. They were all highly disturbed individuals with little hope of ever living a normal life. It was not something they had ever known.

* * * * *

Ozzie was another regular patient on this ward. Now in his sixties, he had spent more than thirty years in prisons and mental institutions like Broadmoor. I had no idea what crime he had committed to end up in that place – something heinous no doubt, but he wasn't the kind of character you could hold a conversation with to ask. He gave me the creeps, as did most of the lifers in there. They appeared devoid of human life, their vital energy long since having snuffed out, their eyes were hollow and dead.

Ozzie spent his day slowly shuffling round and round the snooker table, staring at nothing, speaking to no-one, just endlessly circling. I looked at him and found it hard to believe that he was a human being, who once laughed, loved and had a future to look forward to. Now, with no hope of release or living a normal life, he was no more than a caged and drugged animal who could not have survived outside the walls of this institution anyway. Years of captivity, tranquilising drugs and absence of a loving home environment had stripped these men's souls bare - only the evil that had stolen their lives remained evident.

* * * * *

From the window one day I watched as a coffin was carried out into the courtyard where a special prison hearse waited, armed and guarded. Having been in the dungeon for nearly three weeks I hadn't heard what had happened, that someone had died. I asked the nurse who was in the box and was told it was one of the patients who had been there for thirty-five years. He had died of old age.

The brief relief of being set free from solitary confinement was quickly replaced with utter panic. Mental imagery of being carried out in a box, a withered and decaying man, as mad as a box of frogs, was scarily real in my mind. Adrenalin surged through my body and the usual fight or flight response kicked in at the thought of being caged and trapped forever. I looked all around me and it suddenly dawned on me that I was surrounded by mad, evil nutters. What the hell was I doing here? I had to get out - and preferably not in a coffin in thirty year's time.

* * * * *

Sunday mornings I was able to go to Mass, not to worship but to get a break from the madness and screams of demented men locked in the rooms of the long corridors. The chapel was always packed, and in the front pew sat Doctor Patrick McGrath, the head psychiatrist with his family and behind him sat Jimmy Savile and his mother 'The Duchess' as he always fondly referred to her. The rest of the chapel was filled with patients, some who had been abused in Catholic schools and institutions, still totally loyal to an organisation that had caused them, and so many others, misery and suffering for far too long.

Then one day something happened which would prove to be a catalyst for positive change and would gradually turn my life around. A quiet, male nurse called Ron said he would like to talk with me in the staff office. Over a cup of coffee he invited me to talk about why I was there. He confided how disgusted he was having read the records of patients responsible for despicable crimes, and he said he knew that I was not one of those people. He could not understand the way I was behaving – I was only harming myself and he wanted to know why I was self-destructing.

The nurses and staff were supposed to be objective when it came to discussing the crimes of the patients, but most found it impossible to hide their opinions about the paedophiles. Today, Human Rights activists would be horrified to hear how they were then addressed in Broadmoor. They were consistently referred to and addressed to their faces as 'Filthy Nonces'.

Ron believed that many of the patients deserved to be there because of their terrible crimes. He had looked closely at my records and realised that my crimes were not so bad. He said he suspected I had been the victim of childhood abuse and offered me the opportunity to talk about it. He said that I didn't have to carry on in the same way and that I had a good chance to live a normal life in the future if I was willing to help myself. I felt Ron was on my side and that he wanted to help me.

So, for the first time ever I began to talk about the dramatic changes that occurred in my childhood: the utopia of working on the farm and a happy home life, followed by the seemingly innocent incident of possession of a firearm used to shoot pigeons, which led to my virtual incarceration at St Vincent's.

I spoke about the beatings, the fear of being in a room with four mentally disturbed men who called themselves 'Brothers of Christ'. He listened intently as I told him of the trauma and nightmares I had continually suffered since the age of thirteen. It was difficult at first, finding the words to describe how I had been forced to lie naked on the floor, screaming for mercy while being brutally attacked. I talked for about forty minutes, but I had not told him everything. There was so much more and he asked me if we could continue the following day.

The next day I continued my story where we had left off. I relived the full horror of the abuse, confessing my terror and the humiliation of waking at night being sexually abused by a Christian Brother. I grew more confident as I realised I wasn't being judged at all and that Ron believed me. It all came tumbling out and we met daily that week until I had told him everything. I told of how I had been left with a legacy of guilt, anger and intense hatred for those in authority. It felt safe at last to share the buried memories that had burned inside me for so long.

At the end of the week when Ron had got the full story, he said something that many people have repeated over the years: that there must have been some good Brothers at St Vincent's. Well my answer has always been the same, that not one of them acted on our cries for mercy. When we were flogged in the chapel because we doubted Catholic values, not one of them challenged the abuse or the perverted gratification. They all invariably stood back and did nothing.

* * * * *

After talking at some length with the male nurse Ron, I also began talking to the male and female psychiatrists on the ward. Revealing my past was to have a cathartic effect but it was neither immediate nor consistent. My mental and emotional state fluctuated from one day to the next. But in general I felt a little calmer. It was difficult processing some of the guidance I received in the therapy because of the drugs and constant fog we operated under.

Following the unburdening of the abuse I suffered as a child, the internal rage that had burned within me began to dissipate, leaving me with a sense of lightness I had not known for a very long time. I began to see that my anger had served to protect and hide the emotional damage and shame. I no longer had anything to hide and the darkest secrets I had kept locked inside for so long were no longer secret and shameful. Another human being had accepted the truth and these revelations cast my behaviour in a new light. With this understanding came an element of unspoken forgiveness for myself, which led to a sense of peace and hope for my future.

My behaviour reflected this newfound peace and a month or so later I was sent over to a regular ward. Jimmy Savile popped in and we ceremoniously swapped shirts – as promised if my behaviour had improved. It was a real turning point and a moment of pride for me.

* * * * *

It is perhaps worthwhile to pause briefly here and say a little more about Jimmy Saville, the man I felt I came to know quite well in 1968. He was not remotely recognisable then as the evil monster presented to us today in early 2014 by the British newspapers and media. He was without doubt a complex character -- yet I wish to record without any reservations at all that I only knew him as a smashing, good guy.

As already mentioned, I had just settled down to hospital life there after assessment by the kindly doctors in the Broadmoor high security psychiatric hospital. I was at last receiving the treatment I unknowingly longed for and it was working well. And I was told categorically I should never had been sectioned .

One day as already mentioned, while looking out of a window on the ward, I saw Jimmy for the first time walking in the grounds. Then one evening about a fortnight later, a male nurse came into the dayroom suddenly and said: "I want you all to meet a very important person"

There was a slight commotion in the doorway, and in came Jimmy Savile surrounded by staff members and one of the psychiatrists. Of course we all knew him immediately. He was slightly smaller than we thought and although I had seen him on TV on *Top of the Pops* and heard him on the radio, when we were introduced and shook hands, I was very surprised how frail his hand was.

With his jovial expression, bright eyes, characteristic blond hair, perky manner and outrageous dress sense, he was welcomed by one and all -- the governor, doctors, nurses and inmates alike. He was a bundle of joy to be around people, everybody loved him and no one had the slightest suspicion or inkling of the paedophile allegations that have surfaced in the past year or two.

He would entertain us in groups sometimes -- but that was not all. He would at times come into my room and sit on the bed, asking if there was anything he could help with. On different occasions he even wrote personally to my family, reassuring them I was making good progress. We had almost a father-and-son relationship, and he was just the same with many other patients. In short during that time like many others in Broadmoor, I simply loved the man .

On more than one occasion when I stepped out of line and was severely reprimanded or lost privileges, he spoke to the warden on my behalf. Invariably the measures were rescinded and no further action taken. I can only say that during all the time I was in Broadmoor Hospital he never laid a hand on me or remotely made any improper suggestions. As far as I know, that situation was the same with all the other patients. He had the run of the hospital seven days a week, day and night, and came and went as he liked. He would very often visit inmates alone, even violent ones without showing any unease.

When the news emerged of allegations against him of sexual abuse of adolescent boys and girls and a claimed history of over 100 indecent acts including over 20 alleged cases of rape over five decades, I was dumbfounded. These took place often, it is said, in hospital and on BBC premises. On seeing and hearing this news, you could have knocked me over with a feather.

I worked quite closely with him on occasions in that hospital, in the position of entertainments officer. Often, through his unique blend of influence and personality, he brought famous television acts of the time like the dancers Pan's People to entertain at the hospital, which was always a great morale boost for all the patients.We were always amazed that they spared the time and trouble to visit us there.

One afternoon while preparing for a concert, we were in the central hall rehearsing. Sir Bernard Miles the actor and writer was there along with a famous pop group or two and various other celebrities of the day. I remember telling Jimmy I was finding it difficult not to think of the grief and heartache of some of the patients' victims and their families. And during the conversation I plucked up courage and asked him why he spent so much time there. His reply was: "These poor inmates need help. Killers and paedophiles have uncontrollable demons, you know."

I can't help wondering, looking back, if he was consciously or unconsciously talking about himself. I noticed several times that he would go to confession himself in the Catholic Chapel before communion and mass. I can't help wondering now what he might then have confessed to. But I have to emphasise again, my own personal experience of the man was nothing but positive -- and he helped me and others enormously by his repeated presence and influence.

On one particular Sunday morning that is perhaps worth mentioning, after the service in the Catholic Chapel ended, I was sitting quietly at the rear talking to Jimmy Savile about future concerts in which I would be involved with him. It was at the period when I had just started for the first time to unburden myself verbally to the male nurse Ron about my own experienes of abuse at St Vincent's. I confided this to Jimmy and he listened very carefully to all that I said.

When I had finished, he said to me very quietly: 'I will tell you something now -- and I will say it once and never mention it again.' He paused, and with a look of sadness coming over his face, he added: 'I was abused as a child … by someone I trusted.'

I asked him what had happened, but he immediaely changed the subject. In that moment he looked curiously vulnerable, and I remember feeling sorry for him, having been a victim myself .

* * * * *

My story about my meetings and experiences with Jimmy Savile would not be complete if I did not explain how he ultimately played a very important part indeed in late 1969, saving me from a much longer extended stay in Broadmoor. In fact I sometimes wonder if I might still be there now, if it was not for him! I feel sure, in any event. that my stay would certainly have been greatly extended if it were not for a vital intervention by him on my behalf.

After I had spoken to the understanding male nurse Ron, while spending time in 'the dungeons', I had begun to feel really very much better. Confiding in Ron all that I had experienced at St Vincent's and speaking of it openly and fully for the first time was, as already indicated, a big milestone for me. My relationships with other patients there also became more relaxed and as the winter approached in 1969, I was to my delight given a proposed release date that was then some six weeks away.

But one of the other very ill patients immediately became jealous and deliberately provoked a fight with me on the ward. It became very violent indeed and the staff were inevitably drawn into it. Some terrible blows were exchanged, furniture was damaged and I and others were quite badly hurt. As a result I was placed in a locked room and strongly sedated and one or two members of the staff said to me: 'You will lose your release date now, you know because of this.'

I was horrified despite the sedation, and panicked. Eventually after thinking it over and feeling terrible, I asked if I could see and speak to Jimmy Savile. Eventually he arrived and came to the locked room and stayed for about an hour, listening patiently to my story. As usual he was very friendly and I explained to him how I had been very deliberately provoked into the fight by the other patient who was very jealous of my planned release. I finished up literally begging him to help me as I was horrified that I would once more have to face up to staying long term in Broadmoor.

By then that we had become genuinely friendly. This had come about particularly because I had worked with him on the Entertainments Committee when preparing for the shows that he staged there very regularly. Jimmy had gone out of his way to encourge me to act as compere, and even to sing and tell jokes. One of the songs he rehearsed me for had been made famous by Dean Martin. It was called 'King of the Road' and before perfroming that I did not even think or believe I could sing.

I can't remember now the names of all the famous bands and pop groups that came to Broadmoor while I was there, but through Jimmy Savile, I became throughly used to compering and singing and telling humorous stories between introducing the various top-line acts. On one memorable occasion, a song he had encouraged me to rehearse and sing, in a manner of speaking, "brought the house down". This was because there were, of course, a lot of paranoid schizophrenics among the patients and with a deliberate intention to help the audience see the implied humour of the song as it applied to their conditiohn, I was coached and rehearsed in singing another popular song of the time "Everybody's Talking At Me". It had precisely the effect Jimmy Savile had light-heartedly intended and the enormous ovation that followed was the biggest I ever received there.

* * * * *

It was in no small way due to this work we did together on the shows that Jimmy Savile came to my locked room and stayed a long time to listen to my story about the fight. Before he left, he said simply: "Don't worry, I will see what I can do."

The following Monday I was taken before the hospital's chief psychiatrist with a view to being punished. Damning statements were read out by staff members of what I had done, and I feared the worst. But then the head psychiatrist said that Jimmy Savile had made a special approach on my behalf and explained to him how the very deliberate provocation had come about and why – and he said the disc jockey had also added that I had become especially good and invaluable at helping manage the entertainments and shows with him. In fact he had given me nothing less than a glowing report.

I remained very tense as discussions went ahead about what my punishment should be -- and later even had nightmares about what could have happened that day. But it turned out better than I had dared hope.

I did not get released on the first proposed date, but subsequently a new date was set again, not too far ahead, and I knew that Jimmy Savile's intervention helped greatly in that. His speaking up for me played a big part in my release not being cancelled altogether. And all these years later, I still feel a genuine sense of gratitude for his help on that crucial occasion.

* * * * *

The new regular ward was crowded and noisy. It was here that I met the infamous 'Teacup Poisoner' Graham Young, a serial killer who slowly poisoned several people, including his own family, before being caught and detained at Broadmoor under the Mental Health Act. Graham always dressed immaculately in a suit, white shirt and tie and was well mannered, articulate and very intelligent.

Because of this I would often wish him a good day at the office with a smile and a nod. He was an avid reader of scientific and medical texts and spent many hours in the library. Years later at a court hearing it was discovered that this time spent in apparent leisurely study was in fact time spent feeding his fascination for, and improving his knowledge of, poisons, helping him to go on and further poison and kill many more people after his release. He died in Parkhurst Prison aged 42. He taught me how to play chess and was good company – but we never let him make the tea!

* * * * *

I was given a job working in the kitchen gardens which I really enjoyed. Now that the abuse and traumas of my past was known, regular counselling sessions were arranged with a psychologist, a lovely young lady who helped me to realise I could not change what had happened in the past but could learn to accept it and move on. It seems so obvious to me now, but it was only through the counselling that I came to realise that the suppressed pain, suffering and humiliation I had endured at St Vincent's had manifested into rage and anger, changing my personality and affecting the way I viewed the world and those in authority.

I continued to make good progress and in the autumn of 1969, the hospital's psychiatrist said he was happy for me to be released in November. I had spent a total of twenty months there. I guess in a way I was one of Broadmoor's rare success stories.

PART THREE

DREAMS CAN COME TRUE

'Norwich is a place where a graceful cathedral and a massive Norman tower dominate a huge market square, ancient city walls and a tangle of medieval streets; and allies the gentle river Wensum that runs through it, curving from North to East and South.'
George Borrow

During the turbulent decade or so of trauma that followed my time at St. Vincent's, I was always very glad whenever I was able to return to the city of Norwich where I was born. It's central, historic buildings and its generally tranquil atmosphere, linked with the beauty of the Norfolk countryside which is so easily accessible from the city, give it a very special charm which has always been important and soothing to me. After my release from Broadmoor, I felt particularly glad to be back home there again, and I spent my first month of rehabilitation under the care of the Norfok Mental Health Authority's Hellesdon Psychiatric Unit.

During counselling with a pyschiatrist named Miss Tooke, who was in charge of my case, it was suggested that I should write to the Vatican and give them details of the ordeal I had undergone at the hands of the Presentation Christian Brotherhood.

I sent many letters which were all answered at first, and signed by a Monsignor on behalf of the Pope, acknowledging and apologising for the abuse. Miss Tooke further suggested that I should make a claim for compensation and sue the Catholic Church. So I then wrote again to the Vatican outlining this idea and the same Monsignor wrote back again saying, as I recall, that they sympathised and apologised and that "the matter was being dealth with."

But when I wrote back again asking if I would defintely receive some compensation, their answering letters stopped abruptly. Unfortunately, not realising then that these letters might prove to be of importance later, I did not carefully retain them and no longer have them. I was much more concerned, I suppose, with the immediate challenges of sorting out my life and my future.

CHAPTER FOURTEEN
MY LIFE GETS BETTER

'My own recovery was ongoing during the course of my twenties and thirties and the responsibility of dependants was not manageable for me during this time'.

I remained under the care of the Norfolk Mental Health Authority for a year after my discharge from Broadmoor and continued to receive counselling under the care of a Dr Abel, a gentle and kind psychiatrist who continued my treatment by listening to me talk. With his help I found work as a cleaner at the Norfolk and Norwich Hospital and rented a small flat in the centre of the city.

One evening I went to a dance at the hospital's social club. I was very shy with girls but managed to sit and talk to one of the nurses that I had come to know while cleaning the wards. We talked until after midnight and arranged to meet the following weekend for a quiet drink.

I was nervous but the date went well and we met again two or three times a week. After about a month she asked me why I had not made any sexual advances. I couldn't speak the truth – of the abuse I had suffered as a young teenager, but I realised that my behaviour must have seemed abnormal. With that in mind, I soon took the initiative and made love to her. It was intense and overwhelming, being so close to another person, such a wonderful experience, like heaven on earth. For the next few weeks I could think of nothing else and we made love at every opportunity in her apartment at the Nurses Home. We met during lunch hours too, and her little room became our love nest.

This relationship lasted for about six months until she started talking about having children and settling down together. Emotionally I was not ready for such a commitment. And so we parted.

* * * * *

A few months later during lunch hour in the hospital cafeteria, I met the love of my life, Rosemary, a nursing sister at the hospital. We talked and arranged to meet for coffee in the city the following Saturday. During the next few months our love for each other would slowly grow and grow and only eventually became physical.

"Once in your life I truly believe you find someone who can completely turn your world around. You experience a love you never dreamed possible," sang Bob Marley in one of his songs.

But although Rosemary and I were very happy together, I did not want to marry or have children either. It was not my wish to bring another human being into a world so damaged. My own recovery was ongoing during the course of my twenties and thirties and the responsibility of dependants was not manageable for me during this time. It was not a decision that I regret.

CHAPTER FIFTEEN
SELF RE-EDUCATION

'My education suffered severely during the important years due to my own neglect, and the poor standards at St Vincent's, and I realised that I had a vocabulary of about twenty words.'

With my life back on track after my rehabilitation period and much of the past behind me, I settled into a routine of normal life. I remained close to my family, particularly John and my grandmother's other sons who were so close in age that I thought of them more as brothers. They were all relieved that finally my troubled past was behind me, but they were not aware of the abuse that had caused it, because I still could not bring myself to talk about it to them. Only the psychiatrists and doctors knew of what I had suffered at the hands of the Christian Brothers at St Vincent's.

My uncles, Tom, Eddy, Peter and John were all good roles models for me, having worked hard and made successes of their lives. But it was John – or 'Rocky' as he was known to us, who I admired the most and he was always the first family member I confided in.

Tall, blond and blue eyed, John was an ex-serviceman, fireman and sportsman and much revered in the family as an honourable and caring man. He took me under his wing after my release from Broadmoor and we grew much closer. I was no longer angry and prone to uncontrollable rages but as I adjusted into normal life I was often quiet and withdrawn. Sensing I needed a confidence boost, he took me to Hepworth tailors one day and bought me a smart suit, shirt and shoes. His kindness and generosity were boundless.

One day, fishing in the river Wensum down by Hellesdon Mill, not far from the psychiatric unit where I had been treated on my release, he asked me if I knew exactly what it was that had troubled me so much and turned my life into the chaos of the last few years. I found myself telling him about the abuse at St Vincent's for the first time and how the pain and humiliation had festered inside and eventually erupted. It was easier this time I found. I already knew that none of the abuse had been my fault. He listened quietly and said he would help me continue to get my life back and our friendship deepened further.

John encouraged me to enrol at night school to gain some qualifications. My education had suffered severely during the important years due to my own neglect and the poor standards at St Vincent's and I realised that I had a vocabulary of about twenty words. I worked hard for the very first time and gained seven O'levels and two A'levels in various subjects.

John was always around to help me out with homework, encouraging me to stick with it. When I finally received my certificates I joked that it should have been his name on them. The rest of my family were delighted at my transformation, which encouraged me further. With John's support I was finally able to tell them the whole truth about what had been troubling me during the past years. By filling them in with the missing links and trusting them with the truth, our bond as a family deepened further.

After ten years of studying and working hard and enjoying a settled home life with the support of my loving partner, I had gained enough qualifications to secure a good job as an income tax officer with the Inland Revenue. Again it was John who encouraged me to make this leap from a cleaning operative to an administrative support worker with the Inland Revenue. After several years with the Civil Service I would eventually go on to start my own successful business in the motor vehicle industry.

* * * * *

There is one other very important individual in my life to whom I must also pay tribute who proved to be a rock of loving support throughout all my long ordeals – Nanny Armstrong. In full, her name was Violet Lillian Armstrong and she was the sweetest and dearest grandmother anybody could wish to have.

Because getting a home of their own quickly was impossible for my mother Constance and father Sean in those hard, post-war years after their marriage, they had lived at home with Nanny Armstrong in her council house where I was born. I was five years old before we left there. She once said to me very touchingly after I had emerged from my ten hard years away from home at St Vincent's, in prison, Borstal and Broadmoor: "My one wish in life is to see you recover fully from all your difficulties." And she did, because by the time she died in 1980 I had got myself fully back on track. And in all this she was an enormous help.

During all the time I was away from home, without fail she wrote three letters a week to me which were an invaluable support. The letters were invariably positive and cheerful and gave me all the news about what was going on at home. They were a real and unbroken lifeline to me during all those dark days.

Nanny Armostrong was 71 years sold when she died just before the Christmas holidays in 1980. It was a cold winter's afternoon and she was taken to the Norfolk and Norwich Hospital with a massive stroke. She then suffered a series of heart attacks and the doctors and nurses were eventually unable to help her. The last rites were administered by a Father O'Brien and many members of the family, including myself, were with her at the end when she finally passed.

She had suffered the great wartime hardship of losing her beloved Irish-born husband Thomas who was killed on the docks in Liverpool in a masive munitions explosion. This had led to a breakdown during which all her children including John, my mother Constance and my other uncles John, Thomas, Edward and Peter had to be cared for in a local wartime children's home. Yet after recovering, she was invariably brave and determined and always remained the stalwart central focus of the re-united family.

Her funeral was held on a cold frosty winter's morning beneath an overcast sky at the Bowthorpe Earlham Road Cemetery in the Catholic Chapel which was overflowing for the occasion with neighbours friends and relatives. I was among her coffin bearers along with John and his brothers. I remember vividly listening as the liturgy was recited in celebration of her life, and singing the hymns *Abide with Me, The Old Rugged Cross and All Things Bright and Beautiful.* Then we carried out the polished wooden coffin, high on our shoulders and lowered it reverently into the frozen earth. The family Bible, my grandfather's photograph and a rosary were also carried with the coffin and there was not a dry eye among us as a Father Robson gave the final blessing, and we said our last goodbyes.

Nanny Armstrong, we all agreed, had left behind the greatest gifts anybody could leave – a legacy of love and kindness, not just to her children but to everybody and every living creature she ever encountered in this often cruel world. She had all her life asked little for herself and was for us all a beacon of holy goodness who kept her faith to the end.

One of her favourite sayings was "Count not the years, but count your friends as we grow older", and we all remember her very lovingly for that - and so much else.

CHAPTER SIXTEEN
A LATE ABERRATION

'Don't underestimate the power of the guilty mind. Never underestimate self-shame and self-destruction.'

Tim Hawkins, *Hellbound*

Although the nightmares and memories of my late childhood and early teenage years would never melt away completely, by means of studying hard at night classes and then by further hard work and determination, as already indicated, I had retrieved things sufficently to create for myself a reasonably successful standard of living and way of life.

In fact, with the help and support of some good, loyal friends and the several dear members of my family, I felt I had by my early forties made a reasonable success of my life. And as I have already indicated, I had a loving partner for many years, who had a good job as a senior nurse at the main Norwich hospital. Professionally, I was pleased to have become the manager and an equal partner in a Norwich car franchise near the centre of the city, which repaired and bought and sold good quality cars. I had a nice home with my partner, we had no debts, and had even begun saving something for our retirement.

But despite these successes, the after-effects of those early years at St Vincent's had not, it seems, played themselves out entirely. There was still one final 'road to hell' experience laying in wait, ready to pounce. I eventually overcame it after another hard struggle, but it is one which I don't find easy to describe, nor do I feel very proud of it. Even though there is no doubt in my mind that it too, like so many other past difficulties, sprang ultimately from the deep, inner, guilt complexes left over from those dire experiences of my late childhood and early teenage years. I suppose I only include it here very reluctantly because of the feeling that it is best to be fully honest in telling my story.

* * * * *

In the winter of 2011, an event occurred that at the time seemed insignificant, but would turn out to have a fairly devastating late impact on my life and the life of my partner. It began one Saturday after we had been out shopping at a local precinct, Anglia Square. On our way home, we walked past a local branch of Corals, the bookmakers and one of the staff was standing outside smoking. As we passed, he asked if I would like to pop in and have a free go on one of their touch-screen gaming machines.

At this time, other than wagering five pounds or so on the Grand National steeplechase once a year, I had never gambled before. But on that fateful occasion, seeing no particular harm in store, I stepped into that bookmakers' shop -- and immediately won ten pounds. This without my being aware of it at the time, was in a manner of speaking, re-opening my gates of hell.

What I was unaware of then, was that these kind of gaming facilities, known popularly in the trade as Fixed Odds Betting machines, had been manufactured deliberately to be highly addictive. They are in fact dubbed the 'crack cocaine of gambling'. Unlike ordinary fruit machines found in pubs, or amusement arcades, they are high rolling games, and gamblers could then bet up to one hundred pounds a spin, every twenty seconds. There have been efforts to reduce this recently because of the often-pernicious effects they have had on so many people who have been drawn to play on them.

During the following weeks, I began to spend an hour each evening playing virtual roulette. The staff in all the bookmakers I went into, confided that since the introduction of these Fixed Odds machines they were seeing many lives financially ruined. People were losing everything that was near and dear to them, their earnings, their savings, even in some cases their homes and families. Fixed Odds machines in fact were turning the people who played on them regularly into nothing less than betting drug addicts, who would soon find themselves doing almost anything to fund their addictions.

But like many of them, I believed it could never happen to me.

* * * * *

At the start I began to lose about a hundred pounds a week. But by the end of that year my betting habits had gone right out of control and I had become totally addicted to this form of gambling. The craving was horrendous and I was now chasing all the losses, trying to win them back. As the addiction escalated, the stakes increased, and before long, I was often wagering a hundred pounds a spin. It had taken over my whole life. All our savings were gone – but because of my good personal and car business financial track record, I was allowed to borrow heavily from my bank.

All this too, was leaving me in a permanent state of anxiety and chronic depression. In desperation I provided many photographs for a protection system that was supposed to 'self exclude' me from all the different bookmakers' branches in East Anglia. But, in the event, I was always allowed back in, and the staff of the various betting shops admitted that these government approved self-exclusion systems were really inoperable, and that nobody was able to police them.

I tried hypnosis, counselling, and even prescribed medication – but all to no avail. By 2013 I had lost almost everything we had worked so hard for. I had also borrowed money against our house and sold my share of the car business to pay off all the debts. I spoke eventually of my experience in local television and radio interviews, hoping to warn others away from the problem. And I also contacted the Liberal Democrat MP for Norwich South, Simon Wright who I discovered had become concerned about other victims in the same situation.

He raised my story in debates about these Fixed Odds betting scandals in the House of Commons, and in late 2013 he wrote an article about my case and put it up online, specifically for politicians from all parties and interested members of the public to read across the country. In effect this form of gambling being available so easily has come to be seen by many as a national scandal and Simon Wright's involvement is part of an effort to bring a greater regulation to this area of the U.K. gambling world

I now know that since the relaxation of the gambling laws that took place under the supervision of the Labour Government of Tony Blair, the proliferation of these Fixed Odds betting terminals has lead to much misery and suffering. Hundreds, and possibly thousands of vulnerable families have suffered nationwide. Stories about such cases have made big headlines in the tabloid press, particularly. And my own story in particular was featured in our local Norwich newspapers.

I also know for certain, that somehow, the deeply buried feelings of guilt dating from my early life played a crucial part in my allowing myself to get drawn into this desperate situation, and not to be able to resist it or fully shake it off for so long.

In fact perhaps I should say that for some months before I became addicted to these gaming machines in 2011, to my surprise, I had found myself suffering yet another renewed bout of guilt feelings, worthlessness and depression about my early years. I later learned, through further psychological treatment, that this was completely normal. But at the time, unknown to those around me, I was again turning to alcohol –and this time gambling too -- for comfort.

And I got very heavily into debt borrowing via bank overdrafts, but kept it away from my family. By the time Rosemary, my partner and my uncle John found out, I was in debt to the tune of some £40,000, all of it gone on the Fixed Odds betting terminals.

Eventually I went to Gamblers Anonymous and they were very helpful, saying it was a compulsive thing, which could be overcome with counselling and the right medication. To help myself focus, I joined a local Keep Fit club, went running and walking daily in all weathers and also most importantly came to realise that to neglect, ignore and deny the spiritual aspects of life is a very serious omission. It is vital, I realised, always to live life as fully as possible

During that time I was led to read two very important books in the realms of philosophy and sociology – *The Power of Now* by Eckhardt Tolle and *The Law of Attraction* by Esther and Jerry Hicks. Understanding fully for the first time the importance of living fully in the present moment and not allowing myself to be constantly haunted by my past,or an unknown future, proved to be a great and major turning point for me.

I can hardly bear to admit that, in all, my losses in the end amounted to well over £50,000. That was possibly why my case was chosen for publicising by local M.P Simon Wright.

That setback was a very severe blow to me. Yet somehow, drawing on the inner strength that I had learned to muster in my recovery from my earlier troubles, I somehow managed to pull through again to my present position of quiet contentment with a life that has perhaps seen more than a fair share of ups and downs.

CHAPTER SEVENTEEN
REFLECTIONS IN TRANQUILITY

'The first step to my recovery was to forgive myself, to unload the unnecessary guilt that children often bear following abuse, and the feeling that somehow the abuse was all, or partly, my fault.'

I will never know what kind of man I would have grown up to be if I had not gone to St Vincent's. In life, our achievements are often measured by the quality of our relationships. Our successes are measured by how brightly we shine, or stand out from the crowd, or how we engage with others.

These values and continued successes largely depend on a framework of trust that is developed when we are children and which is continually referred to as we continue through life interacting with other adults who we depend on for fulfilment of our needs and nurturing as human beings. In an average, ideal childhood we learn that adults are there to take care of us, to help us to learn and to grow into balanced, well adjusted and contented adults. I suppose we unconsciously learn to emulate them.

The adults who cared for us as children, often unwittingly and often absently, taught us how to relate, and whether or not to trust or to engage with others. We are prepared to be pushed out into a world that we hope values and welcomes our arrival and is a safe and emotionally nourishing environment. In therapy I learned that none of the abuse or the sickening events of my childhood were my fault, that there was nothing I could have done to have prevented the attacks. The first step to my recovery was to forgive myself, to unload the unnecessary guilt that children often bear following abuse, and the feeling that somehow the abuse was all, or partly, my fault.

Self-forgiveness didn't happen overnight. For me it was more of a slow realisation over the passing of time and the continual reassurance from the professional therapists that my violent behaviour and explosive temper was not a part of my nature but a defence mechanism and human reaction to a series of unrelenting injustices to my soul. Without the professional advice I received, I believe I might still be behind bars, or worse, have become a lifelong patient of a mental institution like Broadmoor, pacing the rooms like a crazed and disturbed animal, never finding peace or freedom. Psychotherapy wasn't an overnight solution to the problem because of my deep mistrust of anyone in authority which has never, ever left me completely, if I'm truly honest.

Since my release from Broadmoor there has only been one relapse into previous learned behaviour of violent rebelliousness against authority - an isolated revisit to a past I thought I'd wrapped up and put behind me. The event was almost an exact replica of an incident I was jailed for in 1966, which had been triggered by alcohol after a Christmas party and I was caught attacking a policeman for no apparent reason other than I was drunk. To me he was in authority and I was still angry. I was extremely fortunate the second time to be let off with a conditional discharge and I made sure I never touched alcohol again.

*****

But looking back at my life to date from a perspective of relative tranquillity, other than a resigned acceptance of my suffering, what have I gained? Surely you, the reader, will be wondering if I have managed to forgive my perpetrators and the Catholic Church?

To the outside world, St Vincent's appeared like any normal approved boarding school and the children were cared for by Catholic teachers whose own education had been heavily invested in. It was automatically assumed that the children's futures would be saved and transformed for the better. Reality, however, painted a different picture.

I so desperately wanted to put the past behind me and to pick up a normal, happy carefree life of a man who had not suffered abuse as a child, but deep in my heart I knew this man could never be. I began to realise that if I were to live with it comfortably then I had to forgive. It wasn't an easy decision, wasn't a decision at all. It became a matter of survival, to live life in peace at any rate.

My lifelong friendship with Father Manley and the unwavering faith of my Nanny and close family had already taught me that not all Catholics were cruel and twisted. I began to ask why the Brothers had been capable of such abuse. I began to wonder how many more had suffered? As it happens, I didn't have to look too hard to find the truth. It appeared that there were thousands more like me, hundreds more like Nutter Arnold in many institutions all over the world and pretty soon the media would reveal the truths for all to make their own judgments. The evidence has unfolded before the nation's eyes with each new headline and exposé. These educated 'men of God' were twisted and sadistic, capable of heinous and violent crimes against the children they were meant to 'save'. And the very sacredness of the supposed celibacy these men were supposed to practice was in fact the origin and cause of their twisted and sick behaviour.

As a man, I would realise the truth; that the Catholic Church creates an unnatural environment where men and women are sexually repressed, which then manifests itself in cruelty and sexual abuse of children. The Catholic Brothers were men who had poor psycho-sexual development and were unfit to be in charge of boys. Many of their victims were often a long way from home, emotionally deprived and vulnerable to assault. Coming from a poor but good and decent home, I knew the abuse was abnormal and terribly wrong, but many younger boys had never known a normal family life and grew up believing it was normal. It is commonly accepted that the abused often become abusers themselves. I witnessed this first hand when I ran into several of my classmates from St Vincent's during my stay at Broadmoor. Sadly for most, they did not recover and would never go on to lead the normal life that I have.

I learned recently during research for this book that child abuse at St Vincent's had improved a little after the 1960s – whatever must it have been like for the children before me, I cannot bear to even think about. However despite the abuse and trauma I suffered, I feel like one of the lucky ones because of the professional and sympathetic counselling I received that thankfully changed my life for the better. Out of adversity, the help I received allowed me eventually to make a wonderful success of my relationships and career.

* * * * *

Meeting Rosemary at the hospital where I worked shortly after leaving Broadmoor was a wonderful experience -- but I never realised at that time, it would become a lifelong friendship and we would become soul mates.

We lived together for a number of years after our initial meeting and along with John, my uncle, she helped me tremendously with furthering my education. Frequently we would stay up late into the night, reading together everything from Shakespeare, Thomas Hardy, Earnest Hemingway, and other wonderful authors. And we also attended night school together. Rosemary had a good education and sound qualifications and came along with me to give her support, for which I will always be eternally grateful.

After a few years we drifted apart somewhat, but still remained good friends. Rosemary set up her own home, and we later lived there together for a number of years; but I also kept my own separate home going and we both liked it that way.

Up until the time I became addicted to the Fixed Odds betting machines, however, our relationship had become really close again and we had been living at my home together for about ten years.We used to jokingly say that we were then in effect 'growing old together' and we were very happy about it, and looking forward to enjoying retirement.

But the betting addiction became so intense and out of control that it deeply affected everything we had worked so hard for and we sadly parted again. However, now that I have overcome the betting addiction, as this book goes to print, we are both talking again about living together once more.

Rosemary has always supported me in her own special ways with my writing of this book and remains saddened by my early life experiences. But in her own words,in the end, she feels it is 'a story that needs to be told.'

* * * * *

As an adult I have learned that the Catholic Church did not stand up for the rights of children unless somebody made them. Time and time again this has been made abundantly clear. The abuse we had to endure was clearly running parallel in Catholic schools and institutions worldwide.

I believe there is a misconception that an approved school is a place for young criminals. This is not always so and certainly wasn't the case at St Vincent's. Most of the children at St Vincent's had been living in overcrowded and impoverished conditions. Many, like me had no father at home or came from a children's home. Older children who were not fostered out, were sent to St Vincent's or one of the five other schools in the country run by the Catholic Church where they stayed until they were sixteen. Already emotionally damaged and disturbed, these young people were put in the care of psychologically disturbed men.

The nightmares and memories of my childhood abuse remain forever as vivid as the day they happened. From this there is no escape, but with professional help I have learned to accept them and can still function as a normal and decent human being. My heart goes out to the thousands of victims who have not found the professional help that I had, and will probably suffer a lifetime of guilt, depression, self-doubt and anger.

If my story reaches just one of those victims, I hope to inspire him or her to seek help to believe in themselves again. What happened to me must never happen again to any child. But I did overcome the trauma and I believe others can do the same in the end if they take a deep breath and start the vital process of talking about it to others.

CHAPTER EIGHTEEN
THE TRUTH ABOUT THE CATHOLIC CHURCH

'The Ryan Report, chaired by Judge Sean Ryan, found that molestation and rape of boys was endemic in facilities run by the Christian Brothers for decades.'
The Ryan Report, 2009

In 2009 the Irish Government finally published its findings following a ten year investigation of allegations of child abuse in Catholic institutions in Ireland. This report is commonly known as the Ryan Report, a two thousand six-hundred page report into child abuse which drew on the testimony of thousands of former inmates and officials from more than two hundred and fifty Catholic-run institutions.

It concluded that hundreds of vulnerable and innocent children in such institutions suffered sexual abuse, rape, public humiliation and beatings. The investigations went back as far as 1936. The Ryan report revealed that Catholic authorities, including inspectors, regularly concealed crimes of a paedophilic nature in those Catholic-run institutions, leaving them unreported and the paedophiles free to continue acts of abuse. The report chaired by Judge Sean Ryan found that molestation and rape of boys was endemic in facilities run by the Christian Brothers for decades. The British newspaper The Guardian, described the abuse as 'the stuff of nightmares', citing the adjectives used in the report as being 'particularly chilling, systemic, pervasive, chronic, excessive, arbitrary and endemic'.

The Congregation of Christian Brothers is a Roman Catholic lay congregation that was founded in County Cork in Ireland in 1802 for the purpose of educating poor Catholic boys in the immediate area. It later expanded worldwide. Its founder was Edmund Ignatius Rice a wealthy local businessman. In March 1998 the Congregation of Christian Brothers published a full page advertisement in the Irish newspapers apologising to former pupils who had suffered abuse while in their care and expressed their deep regret. The investigations didn't stop in Ireland. It was discovered that in Australia, child migrants were sexually exploited on a daily basis. The Ryan Report also concluded that:

- From 1912 to 1970 boys born to single Catholic mothers in England were shipped to Australia and these child migrants were sexually exploited on a daily basis. In Ireland in 2009 after a nine-year investigation, it was proven in a report chaired by court judge Sean Ryan that Catholic nuns and priests terrorised thousands of boys and girls. Government officials and even inspectors failed to stop the beatings and humiliation.

- Up to thirty thousand children were sent to Ireland's austere network of industrial type reformatories and orphanages and hostels from 1930 until the last facilities shut in 1990. The report stated that molestation and rape was endemic in boys facilities run by the Christian Brothers

- Testimony had demonstrated beyond a reasonable doubt that the entire system treated children more like prison inmates and slaves than people with legal rights and human potential. The report said that some religious officials encouraged ritual beatings and consistently shielded their Order amid a culture of self-serving secrecy, and government inspectors failed to stop the abuse.

- Thousands of Irish children at Christian Brothers' institutions were abused and more allegations were made against the Irish Christian Brothers than against all other male religious orders combined.

The Catholic Church have accepted the allegations were correct adding that they were deeply sorry for the hurt they caused, not just for the mistakes of the past but for the inadequacy of their responses over the years. The unprecedented advertising campaign on behalf of the Christian Brothers mentioned above, also provided helpline numbers for former pupils to call if they needed help. In recent years the Sisters of Mercy nuns, who ran workhouse-like institutions in Ireland, offered to pay compensation of one hundred and sixteen million pounds to hundreds of victims who had suffered abuse by their own hands.

When confronted with the scale of the abuse, the Catholic religious authorities responded by moving offenders to other locations where they were free to abuse again. Known clerical paedophiles were allowed to baptise innocent newborn babies. It appears as though the followers of the Catholic Church have been blinded by their faith and have refused to believe the truth about the abuse that has been carried out on a global scale and victims have been numbered in their thousands. We believe that the Pope apologised to victims because he was made to. Those in authority at the time could have stopped the abuse at any time, saving thousands of victims; but their only interest was in living a life of splendour and preserving their own power and glory.

The financial losses of the Catholic Church for compensation will run into billions. By the end of the 1990s it was estimated that globally more than a half billion dollars was paid in jury awards, settlements and legal fees, and these figures grew to about one billion dollars by 2002. As of March 2006, dioceses in Australia had paid out of court settlements to victims totalling 1.5 billion dollars.

By 2009, U.S. dioceses had paid out more than 2 billion dollars in abuse related costs. In many instances dioceses were forced to declare bankruptcy as a result of the settlements.

In 2010, Doctor Kathleen Turner of the U.S. Conference of Catholic Bishops said the crisis was not yet over because thousands of victims in the country were still reporting past episodes of abuse. But the main difficulty revolved around the fact that there was still a general denial that the problem existed at all - and the Church was still reluctant to deal openly with the nature and extent of the abuse.

Although nationwide enquiries of clerical abuse have only been conducted in Ireland and in America, cases of clerical sexual abuse of minors have been reported and prosecuted in Australia, New Zealand

and other countries. Since 1995, over one hundred Catholic priests from various parts of Australia have been convicted of sexual abuse. In America many Catholic priests are in jail and many have been forced to resign. Some live in retreat houses that are carefully monitored and sometimes locked.

* * * * *

Much of the wealth of the Catholic Church was donated by good people in good faith and I believe that this money could have been used for better causes. As children, we willingly handed over a portion of our pocket money to the Sunday collection plate. Little did we realise that the Catholic Church was already one of the wealthiest organisations on the earth.

The Catholic Church is, I believe, responsible for the rape, mental and physical torture of more children, the murder of more women and the torture of more innocent people than any other organisation ever devised by man.

From its inception up to this very day the Roman Catholic Church has suppressed knowledge and fought progress; they openly supported slavery, racism, fascism and sexism and were allies of Hitler and Mussolini. They published the 'Witches Hammer' - a how-to guide to torture and murder innocent women; they tortured and murdered multitudes in the Inquisition and the Crusades – all in the name of a loving God.

Pope John Paul II failed time and again to take decisive action in response to clear evidence of a criminal underground in the priesthood – a subculture that sexually traumatised thousands of youngsters. He offered no outreach to victims and no binding policy to rid the priesthood of deviants. He had a terrible record full of denial and foot-dragging – how can a Pope be a voice for peace proclaiming the sanctity of life and speak for human rights, while putting the church before innocent victims?

During his visit to America, Pope Benedict XVI admitted publicly that he was deeply ashamed of the clergy's sex abuse which had devastated the Church and added that he was also ashamed of the child abuse scandal in Australia, England and other countries of the world. But this same man himself played a leading role in the systematic cover-up of child sex abuse. Before being elected Pope, he was Cardinal Thomas Ratzinger and it was during this time that he instructed Catholic bishops all over the world that when confronted with a heinous act, to put the Church's interest before child safety.

He recommended in a report that rather than reporting sexual abuse to the relevant legal authorities, bishops should encourage the victim's witnesses and perpetrators not to talk about it and to keep victims quiet. The report threatened that if they repeated the allegations they would be ex-communicated.

It has now been well documented that when confronted with evidence of child abuse, the religious authorities policed themselves and responded by transferring offenders to other locations where they were free to abuse again. There was no deterrent and parents did not know they had to protect their children.

All the heinous, despicable crimes against children by the Catholic Church are set amidst a web of power, corruption and lies. The leaders of the wealthiest, most powerful religious organisation in the world could have separated the prey from the predator at any time, but instead they put the reputation of the church and the faith of the followers before the safety of vulnerable little children. In my humble opinion they did the complete opposite of everything that Jesus asked us to.

How did we get to the point where the Catholic Church was allowed any input on anything? It has been responsible for countless wars, the systematic cover up of sustained child rape, the spread of AIDS in Africa and the exploitation of millions of its poorest followers. We need to wake up and realise that our lives, our future and the future of our children and civilisation would be better off without it.

* * * * *

The whole vexed question of child abuse by Catholic priests and 'brothers' has continued to reappear again and again in media headlines over recent years while this book has been under preparation. In February

2014, in hard hitting report, the United Nations Committee on The Human Rights of the Child called on the Vatican to remove all priests known to have been guilty of child abuse from its ranks. It also demanded that the Vatican open the Church's archives so that bishops and other officials who had concealed crimes could be held accountable.

The same U.N. Committee also accused the Vatican of failing to acknowledge the huge scale of global child abuse by the Catholic priesthood, saying that the Holy See consistently placed the preservation of the reputation of the Roman Catholic Church and the protection of perpetrators of sexual abuse above children's best interests.

Belatedly, a few weeks later Pope Francis who succeeded Pope Benedict after his historic resignation in 2013, produced some figures for two consecutive recent years indicating how many priests had been 'laicised' or removed from office worldwide for child abuse offences. This, however, did little to placate the U.N. Committee and at a subsequent United Nations hearing in Geneva in early May 2014 to review the Vatican's compliance with an international treaty prohibiting torture, the Vatican's U.N. ambassador in Geneva, Archbishop Silvano Tomasi. admitted that no less than 3,400 priests had been disciplined by the Catholic Church in the past decade for sexual abuse of children. Nearly 850 of these priests had been dismissed or 'defrocked' between 2004 and 2013 and lesser penalties had been applied to more than 2,500 others who had been 'disciplined for sexual abuse' and 'children had been put beyond their reach.'

Archbishop Tomasi did not dispute the U.N. Committee's contention that sexual violence against children could be considered torture; and he said compensation paid by Catholic dioceses and religious orders to victims since 1950 had amounted to $2.5 billion dollars.

A few weeks earlier, Pope Francis himself, this time in an interview made public by Vatican Radio, put out a personal appeal on the subject. In fact he asked to be 'forgiven personally' for the 'evil' damage to children that had been caused by past sexual abusers among the clergy. He also said 'sanctions' would be imposed. This was described by newspapers as 'his strongest statement so far', but it was also widely agreed by political and religious commentators that if Pope Francis is to restore the beleagured Roman Catholic Church to any semblance of repectability, he will have to deal firmly and effectively with this central issue of historic abuse of children by its clergy.

So although my own experience of these kinds of abuses happened well over half a century ago, this is by no means an 'old' story. This specific deep malaise within the Catholic Church has very sadly persisted unabated ever since – right up to and including the past decade.

POSTSCRIPT

by

John William Armstrong

SAINT VINCENT'S

I

The Unbearable Irony

The stiff, unflinching, wooden stave
Swished through the air, and landed
On the bare exposed back
Of David Michael Armstrong,
Cut into his raw flesh.
And the poor lad,
Just fourteen years of age,
Screamed out loud, in agonising pain;
"Please, please, have mercy! he begged,
"I've done no wrong!"

But his pitiful cries fell on deaf, unfeeling ears;
And five more times the brutal stave fell.
The brothers had their way.
The merciless cruel pain
Flowed from head to toe,
The soft white skin.
Broke open wide,

And the bright red blood
Flowed very freely from his wounds.

Spread like a captive eagle
Upon the cold polished floor,
In the dim, candlelit chapel
Beneath the hanging, crucifed figure of Jesus,
The eerie silence unbroken,
Except by his pain-wracked, sobbing cries.
The cruel twisted faces,
And wicked eyes
Of the holy brothers.
Watched him unblinking,
Their cruel pleasure evident in their evil smiles,
Oblivious to the outrageous irony
That they were performing this shaming beating
With the synmbol of an agonised Christ
Hanging silently above their heads.

David's only crime, his only 'sin,'
Was his 'transgression'
That because of their actions,
He did not believe
In an omnipotent loving deity;
And thus in this fashion
Was the young lad David
Initiated into the sad Catholic Church,
With all its dogmas, popes and saints,
In an awful, daily ritual of sadism
Performed by a brotherhood filled with hatred.

II

Awakening to Forgiveness

Over his early years
David was filled with an anger and despair
That he did not understand.
The body's scars had healed,

But his poor mind was still in turmoil.
Yet gradually, serenely as time passed by,
With the help, love, and care
Of Nanny Armstrong,
And his uncles Peter, Edward and John
And the priest Father Manley, he overcame,
And refused to go down the road
Of hatred, revenge or self pity
That destroys the heart and soul

Very slowly the bitterness diminished,
The window of his soul opened up
To something more independently divine.
The shadows of despair,
He gradually left, discarded, behind him;
He found again the trust and love of his fellow men,
He found his own spiritual path to righteousness.
He read, he diligently worked,
Became a man of good eke,
Surrounded by his family and friends.
He knew deep down and learned again
That there is a soul at the centre of nature.
He learned to place himself
In the midstream of wisdom and love.

And he let this flood carry him to find peace.
He was impelled towards the truth,
To what's really right and what's really wrong.
And has eventually, through true forgiveness,
Come to a perfect contentment,
At last loving himself again
Along with all mankind;
And loving again also, wholeheartedly
The simple and divine goodness
That exists silently and invisibly
Within each and every one of us,
And in all of life.

ACKNOWLEDGEMENTS

My thanks are due first to the Dartford Public Library for providing a photograph of St. Vincent's Approved Boarding School from their archives, which has been used as background for the front cover of this book and also appears among the Illustrations between pages 68 and 77. And I wish to thank Paul Dickson for taking the excellent 2014 photographs of myself and John in the area of the farm where I worked in the late 1950's.

I would like also to express my thanks to the many people who have helped me to write my story. As a novice writer I could not possibly have done this alone, and I have relied heavily on the professional advice and encouragement of writer and publisher Anthony Grey throughout the writing process. Anthony has helped me greatly to cope with the task of giving my story shape and structure. Thanks also to Helen Hart -- now a good friend -- who rescued me from countless stylistic errors, a lot more than just dotting the i's and crossing the t's.

I had first become aware of the name of Anthony Grey, when he was Reuters correspondent in China and was first put under house arrest then later invaded by Mao tse-tung's Red Guards at the height of the so-called Cultural Revolution in the summer 1967. Because Tony, as I now call him, had worked as reporter for the Eastern Daily Press in Norwich at the beginning of his career, there was a lot about him in the local press from the start. Eventually he became the most publicised Western prisoner of the Cold War era and the very first of a long line of international Western hostages, who was eventually held for two long years in solitary confinement before his release in October 1969.

Several British national newspapers called for the UK public to send letters to him in Peking, or postcards from their holidays and even Christmas cards. They were sent either to the Chinese Embassy in London or to the Chinese Foreign Ministry in Peking, to protest about Tony's incarceration. My 'uncle-brother' John had been a personal friend of Tony since their late teens, and John who admired him greatly often said how unjust it was that Tony should be treated so harshly. And of course along with our family and friends we sent many cards and letters to him, but none of them ever arrived. It was once reported in the press that the Chinese Foreign Minstry burned the mail by the sackload.

When Tony was eventually released and returned home, he very quickly wrote a bestselling book entitled *Hostage in Peking*. When Tony returned to Norwich where he had been born to sign copies of the newly-published book, John went to the local Jarrolds bookstore to meet him for the first time in many years and buy a copy. He later gave it to me to read and unable to put the book down I read it right through in one day and a night – and was very moved by the details of Tony's experience.

I later bought my own copy and read it cover to cover many times, finding something very inspiring myself in the descriptions of how he had found ways of enduring the long isolation on the other side of the world. Both John and I were appalled how an innocent man doing his job honestly had been used as a political pawn between two governments.

John and Tony naturally went their different ways, Tony basing himself in London and later becoming a worldwide bestselling novelist. John continued as a local government officer for Norwich City Council and their paths did not cross again for several decades. But it seems fate was to take a hand, because some forty odd years later, while John and I were enjoying a Sunday evening winter swim together at the University of East Anglia swimming pool in 2010, John almost literally bumped into Tony while we were swimming – with much joy!

Unbeknown to us, Tony had returned to the city of his birth to live several years before, and he and John were so glad to see each other again that we all sat down together for half an hour in the café afterwards.

After a lot of initial backslapping and laughter while exchanging stories of their lives, we all made a vow to meet again soon.

And it was during these most heart-warming meetings that John and I began to tell our stories of being educated locally by the Roman Catholic Church, describing the various harsh punishments that went with those experiences for both of us, even at the primary and secondary school level. Gradually I myself began to speak of my own story and Tony was shocked by what he heard. Before long he said: "You should perhaps consider writing your story and getting it into print. A book could be an important extension of your therapy."

Looking back, this seems an almost uncanny development. Tony had set up the Tagman Press publishing imprint over ten years before our meeting and although I did not consider my own story to me anywhere near as horrific as his experience in China, I began the struggle to write it down in detail – and after more than two years it has become this book *Out of the Shadows*. I will always remain eternally grateful for Tony's help with this – and for the circumstances that brought us together in our home city.

And it was with Tony that I looked further and deeper into the whole important question of forgiveness which I had always struggled with off and on before. Forgiveness I suppose I can see can now is the act of overcoming feelings of resentment, or the desire for revenge towards people who have done wrong by us. I believe the weak can never truly forgive. Forgiveness, it seems to me, is an attribute of the strong and the understanding individual.

But with the help of Tony, my remaining negative emotions about St Vincent's Approved School, and the following nine years, were finally erased from my mind. I can at last say that finally, I truly forgave my tormentors – and this immediately made me feel lighter and less burdened. I continue to have a strong feeling of gratitude for this important bit of help.

* * * * *

And I am of course most grateful overall to my family and friends over the years for their support and for always being there ready to help.

I would further and especially like to thank Dr. McGrath, the head psychiatrist at Broadmoor Hospital for arranging intensive counselling at a vital moment in my life – and helping me to learn to live with my experiences and to value my sanity. I would finally also like to thank the nurses, doctors and all the staff who assisted me at Broadmoor hospital.

I would like to thank my dear mum Constance and again my dear Nanny Armstrong, my uncles Eddie and Peter, who often visited me in Broadmoor, and were always ready to help. Very special thanks of course goes to John Armstrong, who knew what my suffering was, and also for his honesty, courage and forthrightness. He was and is afraid of nothing, and has always been cheerful and the fine, steady influence that I needed in my life.

EPILOGUE

by

Anthony Grey

David Armstrong, the author of this unusually powerful book, is a very remarkable man in many ways. He is unassuming, gentlemanly, almost diffident in his normal, everyday demeanour, and also noticeably generous-spirited and spontaneously kind with strangers and friends alike.

When he invited me to write an Epilogue for *Out of the Shadows*, I agreed immediately because it gives me an opportunity to emphasise here some of the rare qualities of both the book and its author. Perhaps the greatest value of the book itself, is that it provides us with a rare and horribly vivid picture of an early-life experience at the hands of Catholic priests and 'Brothers' which sad to say, has been repeated countless times in far too many nations across the whole world. And it has been written with such sensitivity and composure that it gives a very unpleasant subject an unexpected and very readable dignity.

David, it must be said first, is a pleasure to know and spend time with – and we have spent a lot of time together, most often with his uncle, John Armstrong, over some two or three years while discussing and preparing this book. And David takes a lively interest in everything from current affairs, local and national that are covered in the news, in sport, literature, music and art. In short he is a pleasant and very likeable individual whom nobody, at first sight, could imagine having experienced the harrowing and traumatic things he describes so dispassionately in this book.

I have never in my life met any man who seems less inclined, by character or inclination, towards brawling and fighting. So even now, I find it very difficult to associate the David Armstrong I know, with the accounts in these pages of the many terrible and serious all-out bouts of personal violence into which he was drawn, or which he instigated, during his traumatic and undeserved decade in a Catholic Approved School, prisons, Borstals, and ultimately Broadmoor. It seems a near miracle to me that he survived some of these confrontations with his life intact.

So, above all else, I wish to record here the enormous admiration I feel for his successful efforts in overcoming all the physical and pyschological traumas of those hellish years. My admiration is equally great for the very considerable success he also later achieved in catching up – by means of self-designated night school classes taken on his own initiative -- with all the education denied him during the nightmarish, undeserved year at St Vincent's and during its grotesque aftermath. In short, 'quietly heroic' are the two words that always spring to my mind when thinking of how David eventually triumphed over the appalling, long term after-effects of his maltreatment by the so called 'Christian Brothers' at the Dartford Catholic Approved School.

I also strongly feel he has earned and deserved some form of recognition for his dogged and unflagging determination to rise above the enormous challenges presented to him by the harsh Norwich Juvenile Court decision to 'sentence' him to several years at St Vincent's for a very minor misdemeanour. And if no other form of recognition is forthcoming, then this book, I think, will in itself stand, among other things, as a tribute to his courage and determination, and the outstanding resourcefulness he brought to bear in overcoming the massive and daunting setbacks that began for him at the age of thirteen. Submission of *Out of the Shadows* for an annual, national non-fiction book prize is the very least it deserves.

David, in earlier pages, acknowledges handsomely the vital assistance given to him by the loving members of his family, without whose help he might not so easily have prevailed or 'conquered' Broadmoor. And pre-eminent among them has always been 'Big' John Armstrong, in truth his uncle, but because he is only fifteen years older than David, they have both always thought of themselves more as brothers than uncle and nephew.

John has always been a literal and practical 'tower of strength' for David, because he has always 'towered' over most of his friends at around six foot-four inches tall. It was John, with whom I first became friends well over half a century ago. Then we both frequented the same Saturday night dance halls in Norwich, sometimes drank a little too much, and enthusiastically pursued the lovely local girls together !

Today John has creditably established himself with the Norwich press as something of a local poet. He contributes very regularly to the Letters to the Editor columns of the *Norwich Evening News* on matters of local and national interest – but most unusually, he almost always writes, and is published, in verse. And in this book's Postscript, he ably demonstrates his talents in this direction with a very moving tribute to his nephew in verse.

I came to know John in my own late 'teens through another mutual friend, Derek Tyrer, who was a neighbour and attended Heigham House Catholic School with John. It was the fateful, seemingly chance, recent meeting with John – and David -- in the University of East Anglia swimming pool one Sunday evening, that has coincidentally brought this book into existence.

Or are these things really nothing more than coincidence? I was very touched and humbled when David told me during our very first poolside conversation, that he had been greatly inspired in his early efforts towards his own rehabilitiation by my first non-fiction book *Hostage in Peking*, which John had encouraged him to read in about 1970. Although both David and myself had experienced imprisonment and stark deprivation of very different sorts, my two years in solitary in slogan-daubed rooms in the heart of Beijing in retrospect, did not somehow seem anywhere near as harrowing as David's ten years or so of trauma, when I came to know about them in full.

And then only in recent weeks have we both become fully aware for the first time that David's spell in Broadmoor had coincided almost exactly with my two years held hostage by Red Guards in China in the late 1960s. So perhaps there are many things about 'coincidences' that we still don't fully understand.

From our very first conversation, I got the impression that telling his full story in print might not only vividly illuminate one individual's experience of an appalling worldwide phenomenon, but could add something significant to the earlier work David had done successfully on himself in the realms of psychotherapy. After discussing it together, this book additionally seemed like a perfect opportunity to obtain some kind of definitive closure for himself. And having learned from David that the most difficult thing for anybody who has suffered such childhood abuse is to begin to talk about it at all, it became clear how worthy was his ambition, via a book, to help others who had been similarly afflicted. This became the strongest stimulus for both David and his editors, Helen Hart and myself.

Also on another score, I was moved and impressed by the enthusiasm and speed with which he embraced and began to practice forgiveness for all those negative things long past in his life. David has in fact said that when we discussed the idea of forgiveness in detail for the first time, he felt something subtle but very tangible and significant shift in his mind.

Much work is being done today by charities and other bodies in the area of what is known as 'restorative justice'. This school of thought, which teaches forgiveness at its core, brings perpetrators and victims of various crimes together very effectively and is achieving very good results in new ways. My own spell in isolation as a hostage led after quite a few years to a deeper and wider spiritual searching than might otherwise been the case. And my discovery fairly soon after my own release of – ironically -- *an ancient Chinese proverb* had helped me towards an early understanding of the vital importance of forgiveness in coming to terms with such a deeply traumatic experience.

The proverb said: *'To regret the past, is to forfeit the future'*. That first step led me eventually towards a more recent discovery of significant new writings in this area such as, in particular, *A Course in Miracles*, which was published from New York over three decades ago. That book has sold over two million copies in some ten languages to date and is an independent, self-study course in spiritual enlightenment which is steadily gaining a growing following in the United States, Britain, Europe, China and other countries. It places the need for genuine, non-judgemental and persistent daily forgiveness right at the very heart of all progress towards greater spiritual and psychological awareness and wellbeing -- and the effectiveness of this in daily life is very noticeable when carefully and consistently practised. Sharing this became a landmark in the friendship that has continued to grow between David, John and myself.

Here I can perhaps take a leaf out of 'Big' John Armstrong's book, so to speak, and sum up the *Course of Miracles* core teachings in a few succinct lines of verse. Apparently in ancient China, according to Taoist teachings, Chinese scientists and philosphers of that era presented their discoveries and theories in carefully written poetic form...so perhaps John is to be congratulated for reviving those ancient practices in Norwich!

The Whole Truth

See the beauty,
Feel the rapture,
Perceive the joy,
The peace, the love,
Dispel illusion,
Fear and anger,
Live true forgiveness
In your every move;
Be happy, tranquil,
Still and grateful,
Inspire contentment
By teaching truth,
Immortal, sinless,
One with each other
We're all eternal,
And divine, in sooth!

Finally, I should say that I have also been greatly impressed by two further things about author of *Out of the Shadows*. Firstly, the vivid, and precise detail of the memories he has of what was said and done by himself and those around him during those highly traumatic times long ago. And secondly, his unexpected talent for using words tellingly and economically, as well as the calm modesty with which he always relates his incredible story throughout. Little or no 'ghost writing' has been required in *Out of the Shadows* -- only advice and guidance on structure and content. So the book, even in the writing itself, is very much David's own work, and is indeed all the better for that. Might one or two non-fiction book prize judges reach a simlar conclusion? That certainly deserves to happen, in my view.

Norwich
2 May 2014

Anthony Grey is the international best-selling author of the historical novels Saigon, Peking *and* Tokyo Bay *and the recent memoir* The Hostage Handbook. *He founded the Tagman Press in Norwich in 1998.*

BIBLIOGRAPHY

A Course in Miracles; Helen Shucman and Bill Thetford, Foundation for Inner Peace, PO Box 598 Mill Valley, CA 94942 USA 978-1-883360-24-5 (softcover – combined volume third edition 1250 pages)

To Rome with Love - Truth Now has a Voice Michael Murray, Tagman Press, to be published summer 2014

Disappearnce of the Universe - Straight Talk About Illusions, Past Lives, Religion, Sex, Politics and the Miracles of Forgiveness; Gary R. Renard,Hay House Inc California ISBN 1-4019-0566-8

The Way of Mastery Jayem (Jean Marc Hammer) 2009 Santo Christi Foundation Publications ISBN 0-9771632-053495

The Power of Now Eckhardt Tolle, Hodder & Stoughton, London 1999 ISBN 0-340-733500 paperback

The Law of Attraction Esther & Jerry Hicks ISBN 978-1-4019-1759-3

Practising the Power of Now Eckhardt Tolle, Hodder Mobius ISBN 0 340 82253 8

The Hostage Handbook Anthony Grey, Tagman Press ISBN 978-1-903571-46-0

Hostage in Peking Plus Anthony Grey, Tagman Press ISBN 978-1-903571-84-2

The Tagman Press

The Tagman Press was founded in Norwich in 1998 to publish books to help us think in new ways. *Books to inspire, excite and transform* has been its motto from the start. Tagman's founder is Anthony Grey, former Eastern Daily Press journalist and Reuters foreign correspondent, TV and radio broadcaster and author of international best-selling historical novels, *Saigon*, *Peking* and *Tokyo Bay*.

The Tagman Press was merged succesfully from 2006 to 2010 with CLE Print Ltd, a digital print company then based in St Ives (Cambridgeshire). The imprint was then returned to Anthony Grey's ownership. The company is now run in Norwich by Paul Dickson. Sonja Haggett (based in Layer de la Haye near Colchester) is responsible for accounts and distribution.

Best-sellers – Tagman publishes Dr Fereydoon Batmanghelidj, the celebrated non-fiction author of the famous 'Water Cure' series of books. This series includes *Your Body's Many Cries for Water*, which has itself sold over a million copies worldwide and has been translated into more than fifteen languages. Margit Sandemo has sold more than 40 million copies of her enthralling supernatural novels in the languages of Scandinavia, Russia, Germany and Eastern Europe. Her most famous 47-book series, *The Legend of the Ice People* is being published by Tagman (six books to date).

On 11 April 2013 Tagman published a new edition of *The Hostage Handbook*, which contains verbatim transcripts of the secret shorthand diaries Anthony Grey kept hidden from his guards, when he was held in solitary confinement in China for two years, during the Cultural Revolution.

Tagman is also now publishing a 30th anniversary edition of *Saigon* and 25th anniversary edition of *Peking*.

For further information about Tagman's authors, books, e-books,
DVDs and audio CDs see www.tagmanpress.com
To order Tagman books direct contact:
Sonja Haggett, The Tagman Press
Lovemore House, Layer Hall Farm,
Layer de la Haye, Colchester CO2 0ET.
t. 0845 6444186
e. tagmandistribute@btinternet.com
National and international sales are handled by
Global Book Sales, David Wightman
t. 00 44 (0)7963 210830
e. david@globalbooksales.co.uk
The Distributor is Macmillan Distribututuion, Brunel Road,
Houndsmills, Basingstoke RG21 6XS
t. 01256 302592
e. orders@macmillan.co.uk